Slavery and the Constitution

by William Ingersoll Bowditch

CONTENTS.

NOTE.

Page 45 was struck off before I became aware that "Master Auld" now shelters Douglass's grandmother under his own roof. We are glad of the fact, and respect Master Auld for his change. But the case of Douglass's grandmother is by no means a solitary instance of cruel treatment. I might easily adduce others equally cruel, though not told with nearly so much feeling. W. I. B.

SLAVERY AND THE CONSTITUTION.

CHAPTER I.

"SLAVERY AGREEABLE TO GOD'S PROVIDENCE"!

"Thus did Jehovah stereotype his approbation of domestic slavery"!--Rev. President Shannon, of Bacon College, Ky.

"Here we see God dealing in slaves; giving them to his own favorite child [Abraham], a man of superlative worth, and as a reward for his eminent goodness."--Rev. Theodore Clapp, of New Orleans.

Nearly three millions of men, women, and children are held in slavery in the Southern States, not by the ignorant and brutal alone, but by enlightened Christian bishops, ministers, and church members of all denominations; whilst men and women of cultivated minds, refined manners, and delicate tastes, indignantly deny that slaveholding is wrong.

The Right Rev. George W. Freeman, Bishop of the Protestant Episcopal Church in Arkansas and Texas, whilst a minister at Raleigh, N.C. Nov. 27, 1836, preached two discourses on the character of slavery and the duties of masters. In these ("A Reproof of the American Church, by the Bishop of Oxford; with an Introduction, by an American Churchman;" New York, 1846, p. 6) he declared "that no man, nor set of men in our day, unless they can produce a new revelation from Heaven, are entitled to pronounce slavery wrong;" and that "slavery, as it exists at the present day, is agreeable to the order of Divine Providence." The Right Rev. Levi S. Ives, Bishop of the diocese, was present; and, though a northern man, has in writing published that he listened to them "with most unfeigned pleasure"! (Ib. p. 7.) They were afterwards published with the bishop's note of approbation, under the title, "The Rights and Duties of Slaveholders." They were also printed in South Carolina, and distributed gratuitously as a tract by the Society for the Advancement of Christianity,--a society composed of clergymen and laymen, with Bishop Bowen at their head. (Ib. pp. 7, 8.) Rev. Theodore Clapp,[A] the Unitarian minister of New Orleans, says ("Slavery, a Sermon delivered in the First Congregational Church in New Orleans, April 15, 1838," p. 11), "The same God who gave Abraham sunshine, air, rain, earth, flocks, herds, silver, and gold, blessed him with a donative of slaves." Ib. p. 33: "To succeed, then, in putting down every thing like servitude, you must annihilate the word of God." Bishop Hedding, of the Methodist Episcopal Church, says ("The Church as it is," p. 50), "The right to hold a slave is founded on this rule, 'Therefore, all things whatsoever ye would that men should do to you, do ye even so unto them.'" The funds of churches and theological institutions are not unfrequently invested in slaves. Sometimes these slaves are hired out at auction, and from their earnings the salaries of the clergymen and professors are paid! At other times, they are sold in order to change the investment! Thus, in the "Charleston Courier," Feb. 12, 1835, there is advertised for sale, by Thomas N. Gadsden, "a prime gang of ten negroes, accustomed to the culture of cotton and provisions belonging to the Independent Church in Christ Church parish"! ("The Church as it is," p. 72.) No incredible story, therefore, was told by the fugitive slave, who gave as his reason for not receiving the Lord's Supper, "I could not bear to go forward, and receive the communion from vessels which were the purchase of my brother's blood." In the memorial of the Presbytery of Georgia to the Presbyteries of the Southern States in 1844, on the religious instruction of the negroes, it is stated that slaves are "connected with our churches; nay, more, they are owned by our church members and by our ministers."--"What is it," asks the Rev. Dr. Albert Barnes (Sermon in Philadelphia in 1846, "The Church as it is," p. 81), "that lends the most efficient sanction to slavery in the United States? What is it that does most to keep the public conscience at ease on the subject? What is it that renders abortive all measures to remove the evil?... It is the fact that the system is countenanced by good men; that bishops and priests and deacons, that ministers and elders, that Sunday-school teachers and exhorters, that pious matrons and heiresses, are the holders of slaves; and that the ecclesiastical bodies of the land address no language of rebuke or entreaty to their consciences." More evidence to the same point might be adduced, if thought necessary.

This open vindication of the rightfulness of slaveholding is by no means confined to persons residing at the South. In the year 1847, the Rev. Geo. W. Blagden, of Boston, who delivered the last Dudleian Lecture in Harvard University, defended slavery from the Bible, in the pulpit of Old South Church, that second cradle of Liberty! Only last winter (1848), a gentleman of this State, of high legal attainments, at present connected with the Law School in Harvard University, in conversation hesitated not to declare to us his opinion, "that it was not desirable that slavery should cease"! And Dr. Taylor, of Yale College, at the head of the theological department, instructs his pupils, candidates for the ministry, that, "if Jesus Christ were now on earth, he would, under certain circumstances, become a slaveholder"! ("The Church as it is," p. 95.)

Open defenders of slavery are therefore found among the foremost of the leaders in Church and State. And how few of the opponents of the system have a deep, ineradicable conviction, that slaveholding is wrong under all circumstances! Our object is to create and deepen this conviction.

To prove our position, we shall not rely upon the physical condition of the slaves. Notwithstanding the fact is otherwise, we are willing to suppose that every slave is comfortably housed, and has sufficient food and clothing. These may give

"Ease to the body some, none to the mind From restless thoughts."

Even if in a comfortable house, the slave is homeless! No joys cluster around his hearthstone! He has no wife to share his sorrows, or to partake his joys; for neither law nor public opinion sanctions the marriage of slaves! The very children whom the slave presses to his heart are not regarded, either by law or public sentiment, as his dear children, but only as part of the stock of the plantation! Mother and children may be, and are, sold at auction, and separated from him and from each other for ever! And yet the heart of the slave-mother yearns for her children as much as the heart of the white mother.

By giving me a spiritual nature capable of improvement, God has made it my duty to strive to improve myself,--has declared that I have a natural right to improve myself, and that any wanton or unnecessary infringement of this right is a wrong. No man has the right to prevent me, or the meanest slave, from earnestly seeking after wisdom; to prevent me, or the meanest slave, from becoming pure in heart; or to deaden my affections, or those of the humblest slave that walks. In keeping a slave ignorant or impure, or in blunting his affections, even though he is well fed, clothed, and housed, violence is offered to his nature; his God-given rights are infringed; a wrong is done!

Slaveholding is wrong under all circumstances, because it either darkens the minds, brutalizes the souls, and deadens the affections of the slaves, or, without any necessity, renders such spiritual death not merely possible, but almost inevitable. If it is wrong to murder the body, how much more wrong is it to murder the soul! Slaveholding is murder of the soul!

CHAPTER II.

DIRECT MENTAL INSTRUCTION OF SLAVES.

"It is universally the fact throughout the Slaveholding States, that either custom or law prohibits them [i.e. the slaves] the acquisition of letters."-- Report made to Synod of South Carolina and Georgia in 1833.

At a recent annual meeting of the American Colonization Society, the Rev. Joel Parker, D.D. of Philadelphia, a member of the Presbyterian Church, speaking of the instruction of the colored race, is reported to have used the following language:--"There seems to me, in connection with this subject, a beautiful illustration of what Hall calls 'a fetch in Divine Providence.' God had a design in bringing these people to this country in the way he did. We cannot probably comprehend the whole of it; but this we can see, he has secured the education of those who, to all human appearance, would not and could not have been educated in any other way. There are now in this country more than three hundred thousand Africans who can read and write, who could not have done it if it had not been for the slave-trade. There are many in this country and in Liberia who are capable of preaching the gospel, editing papers, and performing all the duties of civil life, who must have remained in total darkness but for this trade. How came this people by all this knowledge? Did anybody go to Africa and teach them? No! It has been done by slavery.... And now we send them back to Africa, with a preparation for doing a great work there, which we never could have imparted to them in any other way.... In this view of the subject, we may perceive at least one good which slavery has done to Africa; and the question may with propriety be asked, whether it has not done for Africa more good than harm."

If we may believe this spiritual teacher, the Being who made of one blood all the nations of men, the common Father of us all, himself designed the scheme by which millions of men, women, and children were torn from their homes and friends, and all they held dear, and brought to this country, through all the horrors of the middle passage, where a terrible death relieved on an average at least one fifth of the victims from a scarcely less terrible life,--for this end in part, that, after two centuries of wrongs, not even a tithe of their descendants might be returned to the land of their fathers, to teach the Africans the religion of their oppressors! A truly touching example of God's loving-kindness and tender mercy to all his children!

That many slaves have been instructed to the extent stated by Dr. Parker is true; but they have been educated, not in consequence, but in spite, of slavery. So hostile to mental culture is slavery, that but a slight examination is needed to satisfy us that it is neither profitable nor safe to educate a slave beyond a certain point. Without some education, a slave would be worse than valueless. Far the larger number of them, as field slaves, are simply taught to use the hoe, and other instruments of agriculture. Others are brought up as carpenters, masons, blacksmiths, house-servants, &c. Frederick Douglass earned a dollar and a half a day at caulking; whilst William Craft, as a cabinet-maker and occasional waiter at an hotel, supported himself, and paid his owner twenty dollars a month for the right to use his own muscles. We occasionally meet with such advertisements as the following, cut from the "New Orleans Picayune," of Oct. 18, 1846:--

"CREDIT

SALE OF VALUABLE NEGRO MECHANICS, &c.--By Beard, Calhoun, and Co. auctioneers, will be sold at auction, on Tuesday the 20th October, at twelve o'clock, at Banks's Arcade, the following valuable slaves:--Ezekiel, 25 years, a superior carpenter, fully guarantied; Jacob, 25 years, a superior carpenter and wheelwright, fully guarantied; Dick, 35 years, a superior carpenter and wheelwright, fully guarantied; Charles, 28 years, engineer and rough carpenter; Charles, 22 years, field hand, fully guarantied, excepting slightly ruptured; Sancho, 26 years, good house carpenter, fully guarantied; Maria, mulattress, 28 years, first-rate washer and ironer, fully guarantied; Maria, negress, 13, child's nurse, fully guarantied.

"Terms: Twelve months' credit for notes drawn and endorsed to the satisfaction of the vendor, with mortgage on the property, bearing interest eight per cent per annum, from date of sale until paid. Slaves not to be delivered until the notes are approved of. The servants can be seen on the morning of sale. Act of sale before D. I. Ricardo, notary public, at the expense of the purchaser."

In the same paper, Alexander Daggett advertises "for sale a negro man, a first-rate blacksmith." In the "Richmond Whig" of Jan. 25, 1848, Benjamin Davis advertises for sale a negro man "who is a first-rate carpenter by trade; also a rough blacksmith." In the "Charleston (S.C.) Mercury," Thomas W. Mordecai, broker and auctioneer, under date Sept. 1, 1847, advertises at private sale--

"An uncommonly prime and likely black man, about 22. A prime woman, a superior washer, and good cook and farm hand. A very prime axeman and field hand. A superior man-cook."

It is not, however, necessary to teach a slave-mechanic or field hand, or even "a prime woman," to read or write, in order to make him or her a profitable investment. If we suppose William Craft's value as a slave to have been two thousand dollars, his master received from his investment only twelve per cent clear profit! Yet William could neither read nor write. He was a valuable working machine. To have him educated farther, to have taught him to read or write, would have lessened his market value. To teach a slave these things is to teach him his rights, and to make him keenly feel his wrongs. Mrs. Hugh Auld taught Frederick Douglass his letters before slavery had hardened her naturally kind heart. She gave him the inch, as he says, and no precaution could prevent his taking the ell. He taught himself to read and write, and thus describes the effect produced by reading a book called "The Columbian Orator." This book contains one or more of Sheridan's speeches, and a dialogue between a master and his slave, wherein the slave is made to refute all the arguments usually brought forward in support of slavery.

"The more I read," he says ("Narrative," p. 40), "the more I was led to abhor and detest my enslavers. I could regard them in no other light than a band of successful robbers, who had left their homes, and gone to Africa, and stolen us from our homes, and in a strange land reduced us to slavery. I loathed them as being the meanest as well as the most wicked of men. As I read and contemplated the subject, behold! that very discontentment which Master Hugh had predicted would follow my learning to read had already come, to torment and sting my soul to unutterable anguish. As I writhed under it, I could at times feel that learning to read had been a curse, rather than a blessing. It had given me a view of my wretched condition, without the remedy. It opened my eyes to the horrible pit, but to no ladder upon which to get out. In moments of agony, I envied my fellow-slaves for their stupidity. I have often wished myself a beast. I preferred the condition of the meanest reptile to my own,--any thing, no matter what, to get rid of thinking! It was this everlasting thinking of my condition that tormented me. There was no getting rid of it."

As a necessary result of his learning to read, Douglass loathed slavery, and detested his enslavers. If he had never read, his eyes would never have been fully opened to the extent of his wrongs; and what is true of him is true of all other slaves. Any slave who can read Sheridan's denunciations of slavery must, like Douglass, loathe his condition, and detest his oppressors.

But a slave who loathes his condition, and detests his oppressors, will be refractory and disobedient. A late writer in the "Charleston Mercury" admits this when he remarks ("William Jay's Letter to Bishop Ives," 1848, p. 12):--

"It has been the policy of this State not to admit the teaching to the slaves, either of reading or writing. We all know why this is so. It needed no great scope of argument to satisfy those who framed our laws, that the expansion of intellect, the hundred influences which education generates, would be very inconsistent with habits of obedience, which was the corner-stone of the institution."

Such a slave will also try to escape at every fair opportunity; and, being able to write passes or forge free papers, the chances for successful escape are very much increased. The owner's hold upon him becomes daily more and more precarious, and consequently the slave's value as property daily diminishes. So true is this, that in Louisiana a buyer may legally refuse to take a slave, if he has only "absented himself from his master's house twice for several days, or once for more than a month." The "Civil Code" (Art. 2496, 2505) declares that the "vice of character," as it is called, which is proved by either of these Acts, renders the slave absolutely useless, or renders his use so inconvenient or imperfect that it must be supposed no one would buy a slave who was known to have this vice.

Every particle of instruction given to a slave beyond what is consistent with his remaining a passive and obedient, working machine, is so much money taken from the master's pocket. Nobody wants to invest his money in a slave who is refractory or disobedient, or who runs away at every opportunity,-- unless, indeed, he buys the stock, in consequence, at very much under par! The value of Douglass as a slave decreased just as fast as his manhood increased; and Capt. Price now candidly avows, that he hesitated some time before he invested seven hundred dollars in William W. Brown; for William was a noted runaway! The love of money impels the slaveholders to keep their slaves in ignorance.

Not only this, but an educated slave, who loathes his condition and hates his oppressors, is an unsafe member of a household or a community. His means for taking a fearful vengeance are ample, and what consideration shall stay his hands? None but an educated slave can plan or head an insurrection. Such are the ones who always do take active part in rebellions. The house-servants constitute everywhere the most educated class. None are more dreaded than they, for this reason in part, and partly because of their living under the same roof with their masters. In a pamphlet published in Charleston, S. C. in 1822, p. 14, by Gen. Thomas Pinckney, speaking of house-servants, he remarks:--

"They are the most dangerous. Their intimate acquaintance with all the circumstances relating to the interior of the dwellings, the confidence reposed in them, and the information they unavoidably obtain from hearing the conversation and observing the habitual transactions of their owners, afford them the most ample means for treacherous bloodshed and devastation. The success, therefore, of servile conspiracies mainly depends on this class for taking off, by midnight murder, their unsuspecting owners; and the late trials, by exhibiting so large a portion of this description among the ringleaders of the conspiracy, afford a melancholy proof of their promptitude to become actors in such scenes."--William Jay's Letter, &c. p. 9.

The love of life itself, the desire for the safety of their wives and children, impels the slaveholders to keep their slaves in ignorance.

Two of the strongest motives which can be brought to bear upon man, the love of money and the love of life, are therefore constantly urging the slaveholder to darken the minds of his slaves. If the former of these motives leads to the commission of so much wrong everywhere, what will not both motives together accomplish to the injury of the slave? But the slaveholders have not been willing to trust wholly to these motives, strong though they are. In many of the States, it is a penal offence to teach a slave to read or write; and, where laws of this kind do not exist, custom, as universal, powerful, and remorseless as the law, accomplishes the same wrong. The following are some of these laws:--

The "Revised Statutes" of NORTH CAROLINA, chap. 34, sec. 74 ("Revision of Stat." 1830, chap. 6, ?), provide that

"Any free person who shall hereafter teach, or attempt to teach, any slave within this State to read or write, the use of figures excepted, or shall give or sell to such slave or slaves any books or pamphlets, shall be liable to indictment in any court of record in this State having jurisdiction thereof; and, upon conviction, shall, at the discretion of the court, if a white man or woman, be fined not less than one hundred dollars, nor more than two hundred dollars, or imprisoned; and, if a free person of color, shall be fined, imprisoned, or whipped, at the discretion of the court, not exceeding thirty-nine lashes, nor less than twenty lashes."

Chap. 111, sec. 27 (Statute, 1830, chap. 6, ?2), provides that,--

"If any slave shall teach, or attempt to teach, any other slave to read or write, the use of figures excepted, he or she may be carried before any justice of the peace, and, on conviction thereof, shall be sentenced to receive thirty-nine lashes on his or her bare back."

In SOUTH CAROLINA, the "Negro Act" (1740, ?45; "2 Brev. Dig." 243), provides that--

"All and every person and persons whatsoever who shall hereafter teach, or cause any slave or slaves to be taught to write, or shall use or employ any slave as a scribe in any manner of writing whatsoever, hereafter taught to write; every such person and persons shall, for every such offence, forfeit the sum of one hundred pounds current money."

In ALABAMA (Statute, 1832, chap. 8, ?10; "Clay's Digest," p. 543, ?24),--

"Any person or persons who shall attempt to teach any free person of color, or slave, to spell, read, or write, shall, upon conviction thereof by indictment, be fined in a sum not less than two hundred and fifty dollars, nor more than five hundred dollars."

In GEORGIA ("Penal Code approved Dec. 23, 1833," 13th div., sec. 18; "Prince's Digest," p. 658; "William A. Hotchkiss's Codification," 1845, p. 772),--

"If any person shall teach any slave, negro, or free person of color, to read or write either written or printed characters, or shall procure, suffer, or permit a slave, negro, or person of color, to transact business for him in writing, such person so offending shall be guilty of a misdemeanor, and, on conviction, shall be punished by fine, or imprisonment in the common jail of the county, or both, at the discretion of the court."

In MISSISSIPPI ("Howard & Hutchinson's Laws," p. 673),

"No slave or free person of color can be employed in the setting of types in any printing office."

In MISSOURI, the "Revised Statutes" (chap. 8, sec. 10, p. 117) provide that,--

"When an apprentice is a negro or mulatto, it shall not be the duty of the master to cause such colored apprentice to be taught to read or write, or a knowledge of arithmetic; but he shall be allowed, at the expiration of his term of service, a sum of money in lieu of education, to be assessed by the county court."

The Act of 1847 (approved Feb. 16, ?1) reads,--

"No person shall keep or teach any school for the instruction of negroes or mulattoes in reading or writing in this State."

Other similar laws might be produced; but these suffice to exhibit, in a clear light, the opportunities presented for the mental instruction of slaves! In some States, it is unlawful to teach even a FREE colored person to read or write!

That these laws have been almost universally respected and obeyed, there is no room to doubt. No one has given more attention to this subject than the Rev. Chas. C. Jones, of Savannah, Ga. In 1842 he published, at Savannah, a work, containing the result of his researches, entitled "The Religious Instruction of the Negroes in the United States." In this work, p. 115, he says, "The statutes of our respective Slave States forbid all knowledge of letters to the negroes; and, where the statutes do not, custom does. It is impossible to form an estimate of the number of negroes that read. My belief is, that the proportion would be expressed by AN ALMOST INCONCEIVABLE FRACTION. The greatest number of readers is found in and about towns and cities, and among the FREE negro population some two or three generations removed from servitude."--As a confirmation of this testimony of Mr. Jones, we know no greater proof that the degraded class in any community is almost wholly uneducated, than that a large portion of the privileged class is so. The law of compensation is divine. We cannot degrade or brutalize our fellow-men, without degrading or brutalizing ourselves. Now, we find that, in the Slave States, almost one tenth of the free white population over twenty years of age are unable to read and write! To some persons this may seem a small proportion; but, in the Free States, with all our ignorance, there are less than one in one hundred and fifty! and Horace Mann, the best authority on this subject, says that "at least four fifths of these are foreigners, who ought not to be included in the computation." In Connecticut, out of 163,843 free persons over twenty years of age, there are only 526 who are unable to read and write; while, in the model Slave State of South Carolina, out of only 111,663 free white persons over twenty years of age, there are 20,615 who cannot read and write! "In South Carolina," says Theodore Parker, "out of each 626 free whites more than twenty years of age, there are more than 58 wholly unable to read or write; out of that number of such persons in Connecticut, not quite two"! More than the sixth part of the adult freemen of South Carolina are unable to read the vote they deposit in the ballot-box! And Gov. Clarke, of Kentucky, declared in his message to the legislature in 1837, that one third of the adult population of that State were unable to write their names! While such is the state of the freemen, it is impossible that any considerable number of the slaves should become educated. With these facts before us, it is impossible not to admit the correctness of Mr. Jones's conclusion. Only an "almost inconceivable fraction" of three millions of slaves can read or write! These are taught by their owners, or with their connivance; and of them we shall speak hereafter. But, taken as a mass, the slaves are truly described by a writer in the "Marysville (Tennessee) Intelligencer" as being "degraded, stupid savages." We may add, not naturally degraded and stupid, but made and kept so in open violation of their rights as human beings, for the sake of gain!

CHAPTER III.

MORAL AND RELIGIOUS CONDITION OF THE SLAVES.

"Their depravity, their spiritual ignorance and destitution, are amazingly and awfully great."--Rev. C. C. Jones's Catechism; preface, p. 4.

"When the charge of the intellectual and moral degradation of the slaves is preferred against us," says Mr. Jones[B] ("Religious Instruction," p. 107), "we are inclined to put the best face on affairs, knowing that this is the darkest feature and the most vulnerable point."

"Their notions of the Supreme Being (ib. p. 125); of the character and offices of Christ and of the Holy Ghost; of a future state; and of what constitutes holiness of life, are indefinite and confused. Some brought up in a Christian land, and in the vicinity of the house of God, have heard of Jesus Christ; but who he is, and what he has done for a ruined world, they cannot tell. The Mohammedan Africans remaining of the old stock of importations, although accustomed to hear the gospel preached, have been known to accommodate Christianity to Mohammedanism. 'God,' say they, 'is Allah, and Jesus Christ is Mohammed: the religion is the same; but different countries have different names.'"

"True religion they are inclined to place in profession, in forms and ordinances, and in excited states of feeling; and true conversion, in dreams, visions, trances, voices,--all bearing a perfect or striking resemblance to some form or type which has been handed down for generations, or which has been originated in the wild fancy of some religious teacher among them." Page 126: "Sometimes principles of conduct are adopted by church members at so much variance with the gospel that the 'grace of God is turned into lasciviousness.' For example, that which would be an abominable sin, committed by a church member with a worldly person, becomes no sin at all if committed with another church member. The brethren must 'bear one another's burdens, and so fulfil the law of Christ.'... To know the extent of their ignorance, even where they have been accustomed to the sound of the gospel in white churches, a man should make investigation for himself: the result will frequently surprise and fill him with grief. They scarcely feel shame for their ignorance on the subject of religion, although they may have had abundant opportunity of becoming wiser. Ignorance they seem to feel is their lot; and that feeling is intimately associated with another, every way congenial to the natural man, namely, a feeling of irresponsibility: ignorance is a cloak and excuse for crime." Page 127: "He who carries the gospel to them encounters depravity, intrenched in ignorance, both real and pretended. He beholds the Scripture fulfilled, 'Having the understanding darkened, being alienated from the life of God through the ignorance that is in them, because of the hardness of their hearts,' Eph. iv. 17-19. He discovers deism (!), scepticism (!!), universalism (!!!)... 'They are wise to do evil; but to do good they have no knowledge.'"

"Intimately connected with their ignorance is their superstition. They believe in second sight, in apparitions, charms, witchcraft, and in a kind of irresistible Satanic influence. The superstitions brought from Africa have not been wholly laid aside (p. 128). Ignorance and superstition render them easy dupes to their teachers, doctors, prophets, conjurers; to artful, designing men. When fairly committed to such leaders, they may be brought to the commission of almost any crime. Facts in their history prove this. On certain occasions, they have been made to believe, that, while they carried about their persons some charm with which they had been furnished, they were invulnerable.[C] They have, on certain other occasions, been made to believe that they were under a protection that rendered them invincible.... They have been known to be so perfectly and fearfully under the influence of some leader or conjurer or minister, that they have not dared to disobey him in the least particular; nor to disclose their own intended or perpetrated crimes, in view of inevitable death itself;

notwithstanding all other influences brought to bear upon them."

"The discipline of colored members is involved, tedious, vexatious, and disgusting" (p. 131). "Excommunications and suspensions are of perpetual occurrence, for crimes shocking in character, and of themselves sufficient to show the general state of morals; such, for example, as adultery, fornication, theft, lying, drunkenness, quarrelling, and fighting. The first three are their most common vices." Page 135: "They are, proverbially, thieves. They bear this character in Africa; they have borne it in all countries whither they have been carried; it has been the character of slaves in all ages, whatever their nation or color. They steal from each other, from their masters, from anybody.... Their veracity is nominal." Page 136: "The number, the variety, and ingenuity of falsehoods that can be told by them in a few brief moments, is most astonishing.... Servants, however, who will neither steal nor lie, may be found, and in no inconsiderable numbers."

Other similar extracts, and touching other vices, might be given; but these seem amply sufficient to justify the general conclusion to which Mr. Jones arrives, p. 153, that "they are, intellectually and morally, a degraded people, the most so of any in the United States; and while, from their universal (?) profession of the Christian system, and their attendance upon its ordinances of worship, and the absence of all fixed forms of idolatry, they cannot strictly be termed heathen, yet may they with propriety be termed the heathen of our land." In a sermon preached by him in Georgia, and published at Savannah in 1831, he calls them "a nation of heathen in our very midst" ("Jay's Letter," p. 11). Abundant confirmation of this conclusion exists. The Hon. Chas. C. Pinckney, in his "Address before the Agricultural Society of South Carolina" (Charleston, 1829, second edit. pp. 10-12; Jones's "Relig. Inst." p. 141), says, "There needs no stronger illustration of the doctrine of human depravity than the state of morals on plantations in general." "Who would credit it," asks the Committee of the Synod of South Carolina and Georgia in 1833, "that, in these years of revival and benevolent effort, in this Christian republic, there are over two millions of human beings in the condition of heathen, and in some respects in a worse condition? From long-continued and close observation, we believe that their moral and religious condition is such that they may justly be considered the heathen of this Christian country." The Executive Committee of the Kentucky Union for the Moral and Religious Improvement of the Colored Race, in their "Circular to the Ministers of the Gospel in Kentucky," 1834

(Jones's "Relig. Inst." p. 143), say, "We desire not to represent that condition worse than it is. Doubtless, the light that shines around them, more or less illuminates their minds, and moralizes their characters. We hope and believe, that some of them, though poor in this world's goods, will be found rich in spiritual possessions in the day when the King of Zion shall make up his jewels. We know that many of them are included in the visible church, and frequently exhibit great zeal; but it is to be feared, that it is often a zeal without knowledge; and of the majority it must be confessed, that the light shineth in darkness, and the darkness comprehendeth it not. After making all reasonable allowances, our colored population can be considered, at the most, but semi-heathen."

In view of these statements, we cannot but be forced to the conclusion, that the slaves, as a body, are in an extremely degraded moral and religious condition. That they are naturally thus, even Mr. Jones denies ("Relig. Instruction," p. 124). He says, "As to moral and religious character, the negroes are naturally what other men are." That they are so much more degraded than others must, then, be owing to their education or their social condition. The inference, therefore, is unavoidable that they have been thus degraded by others. The wrong rests upon those who have denied them the means of education, and who have kept them in slavery,--upon those who have thus degraded their minds and souls, in order that their bodies might remain in slavery! In violation of the slave's dearest rights, all the highest, noblest, and purest instincts of his nature have been destroyed, in order to advance the pecuniary interests of the man "who gains his fortune from the blood of souls"! Are those slaves who enjoy moral and religious instruction any better off?

CHAPTER IV.

MORAL AND RELIGIOUS TEACHERS OF THE SLAVES.

"Q. When you hear the minister preach, are you not to listen to him as the minister of God; God's messenger to your soul? A. Yes."--Jones's Catechism, p. 140.

"By the providence and word of God," says Mr. Jones ("Religious Instruction," pp. 165, 166), "are we under obligations to impart the gospel to our servants.... We cannot disregard this obligation ... without forfeiting our humanity, our gratitude, our consistency, and our claim to the spirit of Christianity itself. Our humanity.... The Lord Jesus has furnished us with the most beautiful and striking illustrations of this virtue:--'What man shall there be among you, that shall have one sheep; and, if it fall into a pit, will he not lay hold on it, and lift it out?' 'Doth not each one of you loose his ox or his ass from the stall, and lead him away to watering? And ought not this woman, being a daughter of Abraham, whom Satan hath bound, lo, these eighteen years, be loosed from this bond?'... Apply the reasoning: 'How much, then, is a man better than a sheep or an ox?' When our servants are sick and diseased, we do not suffer them to want: we physic and nurse them (?). But are not their souls more precious than their bodies? Much more, then, should we lift our servants from the pit of ignorance, moral pollution and death, into which they have fallen. Much more should we strive to loose them (bound for so many years!) from the bonds of sin and Satan, and lead away their famishing souls to the water of life."

"Our gratitude. They nurse us in infancy, contribute to our pleasures and pastimes in youth, and furnish us with the means of education. They constitute our wealth, and yield us all the comforts and conveniences of life. They may, in a degree, adopt towards us the language of Jacob to Laban, 'Thus I was: in the day the drought consumed me, and the frost by night, and my sleep departed from mine eyes.' They watch around our languishing beds in sickness, share in our misfortunes, weep over us when we die, prepare us for the burial, and carry us to the house appointed for all the living. The obligations, the sacrifice, and service are not to be all on one side, in the relation of master and servant. If we have been made partakers of their carnal things, our duty is also to minister unto them in spiritual things,[D] Rom. xv. 27. 1 Cor. ix. 11. And shall we consider it a great thing to fulfil this duty? The kindest and the most grateful return which we can make them is to put them in possession of the richest gift of God to men, the gospel of our Lord and Saviour Jesus Christ."

How far has the existence or utterance of such sentiments as these resulted in securing to the slaves a sound moral and religious instruction? What kind of teachers and what kind of instruction are thought to be consistent with proper feelings of gratitude and humanity on the part of masters? We have just seen the deep moral degradation of the very great majority of the slaves. Still "there are at the present time," says Mr. Jones (p. 100), "tens of thousands connected by a credible profession to the church of Christ, and the gospel is reaching them to a greater extent and in greater purity and power than ever before."

By whom is the gospel thus preached to them in purity and power? Who is it that "ministers unto them in spiritual things," and "leads away their famishing souls to the water of life"?

"Those who would keep the Bible from their fellow-creatures are the enemies of God and man. The Bible belongs of right to every man. It is the property of the world." Thus speaks the Protestant defender of slavery, Charles C. Jones ("Catechism," p. 80). But to prevent a slave from reading the Bible is not by any means to keep the Bible from him! In what a Catholic spirit he thus exhorts the slaves! ("Catechism," p. 79) "What benefit will this precious book be to us, unless we diligently study it, and embrace opportunities of receiving instruction from it, such as are afforded us in the house of God, in the sabbath-school, and in the Bible-class? 'Search the Scriptures' is the Redeemer's command."[E] "We cannot," he says ("Religions Instruction," p. 167), "cry out against the Papists for withholding the Scriptures from the common people, and keeping them in ignorance of the way of life; for our inconsistency is as great as theirs, if we withhold the Bible from our servants, and keep them in ignorance of its saving truths, which we certainly do while we will not provide ways and means of having it read and explained to them"! So readily, at the bidding of slavery, will Protestants surrender the most distinctive feature of Protestantism!

It is obvious, that, if any religious instruction is to be imparted to slaves, it must be given them by others. But it is in the power of the owner to forbid all such instruction. "The whole arrangement of the religious instruction of the negroes, as to teachers, times, places, matter and manner, is in our own power," says Mr. Jones (ib. p. 98).

The Presbytery of Georgia, in the memorial before alluded to, says--

"The law of the land makes and can make no provision for their religious instruction. That instruction is committed to owners, as the instruction of children is to parents; and they can give or withhold it at pleasure. We owners and ministers are 'the almoners of divine mercy to them,' and, if we do not open the door of salvation, they may grope their way into a miserable eternity; for they have no power of any kind to originate and establish and carry forward church organizations and associations for their own benefit. They are entirely dependent upon us for the gospel of salvation."

"We may," says Mr. Jones ("Religious Instruction," p. 158), "according to the power lodged in our hands, forbid religious meetings and religious instruction on our own plantations; we may forbid our servants going to church at all, or only to such churches as we may select for them; we may literally shut up the kingdom of heaven against men, and suffer not them that are entering to go in!"

Wherever an owner is willing to permit such instruction, it must still be carried on wholly by oral communications. "This immense mass of immortal beings," says Mr. Jones, "is thrown for religious instruction upon oral communications entirely" (ib. p. 157). That any oral instruction of the adult or aged slaves is worth but little he evidently admits, because he says (ib. p. 229), "If a people are to be instructed orally, let the instruction be communicated to them in early life;" and "the great hope of permanently benefiting the negroes is laid in sabbath-schools, in which children and youth may be trained up in the knowledge of the Lord." Our minds are so constituted, that, unless our powers of memory have been strengthened by constant or frequent use in youth, we cannot in after-life either receive or retain much benefit from oral instruction. And if this is true of the freeman, how much more is it true of the slave! Consequently, the only method of instructing the slaves, which law or custom or both do not forbid, is the very last,--the poorest method for their real good which can be devised!

There are colored preachers at the South, "and some of them," says Mr. Jones, "are able to read" (ib. p. 175). The following anecdote, illustrative of their capacity to impart knowledge, is told by Charles Lyell. When in Louisville, Ky. he attended a Methodist Church. "The preacher was a full black, spoke good English, and quoted Scripture well." "It appeared," says Prof. Lyell, "from his explanation of 'Whose superscription is this?' that he supposed the piece of money to be a dollar note, to which C鋥ar had put his signature."

Some, probably most of them, are slaves. We have now before us the advertisement of a runaway slave who claimed to be a Methodist preacher! The Alabama Baptist Association bought one of its missionaries, named C鋥 ar, in 1828, and owned him till the time of his death! He lived to be 76 years old. A writer in the "Georgia Christian Index" begins an obituary notice of him thus, "A good colored man has fallen in Israel;" and ends by saying, "The writer can truly say that his labors have been much blest." Mr. Jones gives the names of several other slave preachers. Still, however, they are discountenanced.

The "Revised Statutes" of NORTH CAROLINA (chap. 111, sec. 34; "Revision of Statute," 1831, chap. 4, sec. 1) provide that--

"It shall not be lawful, under any pretence, for any slave or free person of color to preach or exhort in public, or in any manner to officiate as a preacher or teacher in any prayer-meeting or other association for worship where slaves of different families are collected together; and if any free person of color shall be thereof duly convicted, on indictment, before any court having jurisdiction thereof, he shall for each offence receive not exceeding thirty-nine lashes on his bare back; and when any slave shall be guilty of a violation of this section, he shall, on conviction before a single magistrate, receive not exceeding thirty-nine lashes on his bare back."

In ALABAMA (Stat. 1832, chap. 8, sec. 24; "Clay's Digest," 545, sec. 35),--

"If any slave or free person of color shall preach to, exhort, or harangue any slave or slaves or free persons of color, unless in the presence of five respectable (!) slaveholders, any such slave or free person of color so offending shall, on conviction before any justice of the peace, receive, by order of said justice of the peace, thirty-nine lashes for the first offence, and fifty lashes for every offence thereafter; and any person may arrest any such slave or free person of color, and take him before a justice of the peace for trial,--Provided that the negroes so haranguing or preaching shall be licensed thereto by some regular body of professing Christians immediately in the neighborhood, and to whose society or church such negro shall properly belong."

In GEORGIA, the Act approved Dec. 23, 1833, sec. 5 ("Prince's Digest," 808; "Hotchkiss's Codification," 840, 841), provides that--

"No person of color, whether free or slave, shall be allowed to preach to, exhort, or join in any religious exercise with, any persons of color, either free or slave, there being more than seven persons of color present," &c.

In MISSISSIPPI, the law declares (How. and Hutch. 178) that--

"It shall not be lawful for any slave, free negro or mulatto to exercise the functions of a minister of the gospel under the penalty of thirty-nine lashes,-- Provided that it shall be lawful for any master or owner to permit his slave to preach upon his own premises, but not to permit any other slaves but his own to assemble there on such occasion."

In MISSOURI, the Act approved Feb. 16, 1847, sec. 2, provides that--

"No meeting or assemblage of negroes or mulattoes for the purpose of religious worship or preaching shall be held or permitted, where the services are performed or conducted by negroes or mulattoes, unless some sheriff, constable, marshal, police officer, or justice of the peace shall be present during all the time of such meeting or assemblage, in order to prevent all seditious speeches and disorderly and unlawful conduct of every kind."

"Negro preachers are discouraged," says Mr. Jones ("Religious Instruction," p. 157), "if not suppressed, on the ground of incompetency, and liability to abuse their office and influence to the injury of the morals of the people, and the infringement of the laws and peace of the country. I would not go all the lengths of many on this point; for, from my own observation, negro preachers may be employed and confided in, and so regulated as to do their own color great good, and community no harm." Ib. p. 274: "The appointment of colored preachers and watchmen by the white churches, and under their particular supervision, in many districts of country, has been attended with happy effects; and such auxiliaries, properly managed, may be of great advantage." Doubtless, when thus "properly managed," they are of great advantage! "I shall never forget," says Mr. Jones (ib. p. 215), "the remark of a venerable colored preacher, made with reference to the Southampton tragedy" (i.e. Nat. Turner's insurrection in Southampton, Va. in 1832). "With his eyes filled with tears, and his whole manner indicating the deepest emotion, said he, 'Sir, it is the gospel that we, ignorant and wicked people, need.(!) If you will give us the gospel, it will do more for the obedience of servants and the peace of community than all your guards and guns and bayonets.' This same Christian minister, on receiving a packet of inflammatory pamphlets through the post-office, and discovering their character and intention, immediately called upon the mayor of the city, and delivered them into his hands. Who can estimate the value in community of one such man acting under the influence of the gospel of peace?"

Not only are negro preachers thus discountenanced, unless they are the abject tools of the slaveholders, but only a certain class of white teachers are allowed. The following extract is taken from the "Georgia Christian Index:"--

"PREACHERS FOR THE SLAVES.--We think the instruction of the blacks in the South should be committed wholly to white men; and they should be Southern men, in whom the masters have confidence. If the preacher is himself a slaveholder, as are Mr. Jones and Mr. Law, they will command the greater confidence, and have access to the larger number of plantations."

"The field of labor among the negroes in the South," says Mr. Jones ("Religious Instruction," p. 196), "is one, in many respects, of no ordinary difficulty; and it is the dictate as well of benevolence as of prudence to inquire into the character and qualifications of those who enter it. They should be Southern men; men entitled to that appellation; either those who have been born and reared in the South, or those who have identified themselves with the South, and are familiarly acquainted with the structure of society; in a word, men having their interests in the South. Such men would possess the confidence of the community; for they would not act, in their official connection with the negroes, in such a manner as to breed disturbances, which would inevitably jeopard their own lives, and tend to the utter prostration of their families and interests." Ib. p. 235: "The missionaries should be Southern men, or men ... identified in views, feelings, and interests with the South, and who possess the confidence of society." We should (ib. p. 197) "know who their teachers are, and what and when and where they are taught."

The object of these laws and precautions evidently is wholly to exclude, as religious teachers of the slaves, all persons except slaveholders, or those who are fully identified with or subject to them. Only slaveholders and their tools can be "God's messengers" to the souls of the slaves! The moral and religious teaching of the slaves is exclusively vested in that class of men whose interest it is to uphold and strengthen slavery! A slaveholder must have the strongest inducement to make his teaching of such a quality as directly to increase the market value of his hearers; and yet the slaves are receiving from the hallowed lips of their owners the gospel of love and human brotherhood in greater purity and power than ever before!

CHAPTER V.

DIRECT RELIGIOUS INSTRUCTION OF SLAVES.

"Hath He not brought you out of a land of darkness and ignorance, where your forefathers knew nothing of him, to a country where you may come to the knowledge of the only true God, and learn a sure way to heaven?"--Right Rev. Bishop Meade's Instruction to Slaves.

"The religious instruction of your people will promote your own interests for time and eternity."--Rev. C. C. Jones's Teaching to Slaveholders ("Rel. Inst." p. 275).

We might safely presume, that religions owners would instruct their slaves in such doctrines as they deemed essential to the salvation of their own souls, and that such instruction would not materially vary from that given elsewhere on the same points. But abundant proof exists. The Right Rev. Levi S. Ives has published "A Catechism to be taught orally to those who cannot read;" New York, 1848. In the preface, he says it was the result of a winter's visit to a large Southern plantation, and was adapted by him, "in a course of actual experiment, to the capacity of colored children, from four to twelve years of age." There are twenty lessons in this little book. He teaches, among other things, about the fall, original sin, the atonement, the trinity, and the sacraments. Elsewhere ("Spirit of Missions," Nov. 1842) he has expressed the conviction, that, if the planters of North Carolina would adopt it, and see to its faithful inculcation, the next generation of blacks in that State, "at a very small expense, would sufficiently understand the truth as it is in Jesus, without knowing a letter of the alphabet."

Dr. Jones's Catechism is really, what it professes to be, a "Catechism of Scripture doctrine, as well as practice," and contains a very much more elaborate exposition than Bishop Ives's book. Altogether, it must be a much more serviceable book to "owners and ministers."

We shall therefore chiefly content ourselves with showing what the slaves are taught it is their duty to do, and to refrain from doing, and what motives to duty are urged upon them.

"As ministers or missionaries to the negroes," says Mr. Jones ("Rel. Inst." p. 270), "in the discharge of our official duty, and in our intercourse with the negroes, we should have nothing to do with their civil condition. We are appointed of God to preach 'the unsearchable riches of Christ' to our perishing fellow-men. We are to meditate upon the duties and responsibilities of our office, and to give ourselves wholly to it." Ib. pp. 193, 194: "We separate entirely their religious and their civil condition, and contend that the one may be attended to without interfering with the other. Our principle is that laid down by the holy and just one, 'Render unto Cæsar the things which are Cæsar's, and unto God the things that are God's.' And Christ and his apostles are our example. Did they deem it proper and consistent with the good order of society to preach the gospel to servants? They did. In discharge of this duty, did they interfere with their civil condition? They did not. They expressed no opinion whatever on the subject, if we except that which appears in one of the Epistles to the Corinthian Church (1st Epist. chap. vii. ver. 19-23). There the Apostle Paul considers a state of freedom preferable to one of servitude, and advises slaves, if they can lawfully obtain their freedom, to do it; but not otherwise. He does not treat the question as one of very great moment, in comparison to the benefits of the gospel. 'Art thou called being a servant, care not for it; but if thou mayest be made free, use it rather; for he that is called in the Lord, being a servant, is the Lord's freeman,' &c. May we not follow in the footsteps of our Saviour and his apostles, and that with perfect safety too? Yea, and without proceeding as far as did the Apostle Paul?(!) We maintain that in judicious religious instruction there will be no necessary interference with their civil condition. The religious teacher must step out of his way for the purpose." The Presbytery of Georgia declares in its memorial, that, if the church will undertake the religious instruction of the slaves,--

"The minds of ministers and members will be drawn off from abstract questions of a civil and a political nature, with which, as Christians engaged in evangelizing the world, we have little to do; and they will be presented with a way whereby they may practically gratify all their benevolent sympathies for the negroes, in the best manner possible. Our attention, as a church, will be turned to the great question before us, and indeed before all other denominations, and which should take precedence of all other questions touching the negroes, Shall this people be saved or lost?"

"The New Testament," says the Rev. Theodore Clapp (Sermon, pp. 25, 26, and these are his present sentiments), "decides in the plainest terms that Christians are bound to acquiesce in and support those laws and regulations concerning slavery which are enacted by the respective civil governments under which they live. The legislature must determine who shall be kept in bondage, and what shall be their condition and privileges. The pulpit must not interfere in this important and delicate matter.... Let him (the clergyman) at all times preach unconditional submission to civil laws and institutions."

At the outset, therefore, the religious teachers of the slaves disclaim all desire or intention to interfere with the condition of servitude. Their appropriate and only work, they say, is the saving of souls![F] That their brother's soul is brutalized and deadened, in consequence of slavery, is to them no reason why they should interfere with slavery; for slavery is a civil condition, which God, in his mysterious providence, has allowed to exist! But, though it is thus improper to "interfere" with the civil condition of the slaves, that religious teacher (as we shall shortly see) does not "step out of his way," but merely does his duty, who preaches to them that submission to their civil condition, and faithful service for their masters, is demanded of them by God! They cannot interfere to injure the institution of slavery; but very materially to strengthen it falls within their legitimate province! To condemn slavery would be to condemn the providence of God; but in strengthening slavery, they are preaching "the unsearchable riches of Christ" to their perishing fellow-men!

The Right Rev. William Meade, Bishop of the Protestant Episcopal Church for the diocese of Virginia, who has also devoted a great deal of attention to the religious instruction of slaves, a few years since collected and published a volume of sermons and tracts, designed to aid the almoners of Divine Mercy in their work of salvation. The grand motive to duty is thus presented to the slaves, pp. 94, 95 ("Slavery and the Slaveholder's Religion as opposed to Christianity, by Samuel Brooke," p. 29, &c.):--

"Besides, when people die, we know but of two places they have to go to, and that is heaven or hell; so that whoever misses the one must go to the other. Now, heaven is a place of great happiness, which God hath prepared for all that are good; where they shall enjoy rest from their labors, and a blessedness which shall never have an end. And hell is a place of great torment and misery, where all wicked people will be shut up with the devil and other evil spirits, and be punished for ever because they will not serve God. If, therefore, we would have our souls saved by Christ; if we would escape hell and obtain heaven, we must set about doing what he requires of us, that is, to serve God. Your own poor circumstances in this life ought to put you particularly upon this, and taking care of your souls; for you cannot have the pleasures and enjoyments of this life like rich free people, who have estates and money to lay out as they think fit. If others will run the hazard of their souls, they have a chance of getting wealth and power, of heaping up riches, and enjoying all the ease, luxury, and pleasure their hearts should long after. But you can have none of these things; so that, if you sell your souls for the sake of what poor matters you can get in this world, you have made a very foolish bargain indeed. Almighty God hath been pleased to make you slaves here, and to give you nothing but labor and poverty in this world, which you are obliged to submit to, as it is his will that it should be so. And think within yourselves what a terrible thing it would be, after all your labors and sufferings in this life, to be turned into hell in the next life; and, after wearing out your bodies in service here, to go into a far worse slavery when this is over, and your poor souls be delivered over into the possession of the devil, to become his slaves for ever in hell, without any hope of ever getting free from it. If, therefore, you would be God's freemen in heaven, you must strive to be good and serve him here on earth. Your bodies, you know, are not your own: they are at the disposal of those you belong to; but your precious souls are still your own, which nothing can take from you, if it be not your own fault. Consider well, then, that, if you lose your souls by leading idle, wicked lives here, you have got nothing by it in this world, and you have lost your all in the next. For your idleness and wickedness is generally found it, and your bodies suffer for it here; and, what is far worse, if you do not repent and amend, your unhappy souls will suffer for it hereafter."

The Rev. Alexander Glennie, Rector of All-Saints Parish, Waccamaw, S.C. has for several years been in the habit of preaching expressly for slaves. In 1844, he published in Charleston a selection of these sermons, under the title of "Sermons preached on Plantations to Congregations of Negroes." This book[G] contains twenty-six sermons; and in twenty-two of them there is either a more or less extended account or a reference to eternal misery in hell as a motive to duty. He thus describes the day of judgment (Serm. 15, Matt. xxv. 31, p. 90):--

"When all people shall be gathered before him, 'he shall separate them one from another, as a shepherd divideth his sheep from the goats; and he shall set the sheep on his right hand, but the goats on the left.' That, my brethren, will be an awful time, when this separation shall be going on; when the holy angels, at the command of the great Judge, shall be gathering together all the obedient followers of Christ, and be setting them on the right hand side of the judgment-seat, and shall place all the remainder on the left. Remember that each of you must be present; remember that the great Judge can make no mistake; and that you shall be placed on one side or on the other, according as in this world you have believed in and obeyed him or not. How full of joy and thanksgiving will you be, if you shall find yourselves placed on the right hand! but how full of misery and despair, if the left shall be appointed as your portion!"...

"But what shall he say to the wicked on the left hand? To them he shall say, 'Depart from me, ye cursed, into everlasting fire, prepared for the devil and his angels.' He will tell them to depart: they did not while here seek him by repentance and faith; they did not obey him; and he will drive them from him. He will call them cursed."

Page 42 (Sermon 7, Rom. vi. 28): "The death, which is the wages of sin, is this everlasting fire, prepared for the devil and his angels. It is a fire which shall last for ever; and the devil and his angels, and all people who will not love and serve God, shall there be punished for ever. The Bible says, 'The smoke of their torment ascendeth up for ever and ever:' the fire is not quenched; it never goes out: 'their worm dieth not:' their punishment is spoken of as a worm, always feeding upon them, but never consuming them: it never can stop."

Mr. Jones orally catechizes[H] the slaves in the same manner:--

Page 83: "Q. Are there two places only spoken of in the Bible to which the souls of men go after death?--A. Only two.

Q. Which are they?--A. Heaven and hell.

Pp. 91, 92: Q. After the Judgment is over, into what place do the righteous go?--A. Into heaven.

Q. What kind of a place is heaven?--A. A most glorious and happy place.

* * * * *

Q. Shall the righteous in heaven have any more hunger or thirst, or nakedness or heat or cold? Shall they any more have sin or sorrow, or crying or pain or death?--A. No.

Q. Repeat, 'And God shall wipe away all tears from their eyes.'--A. 'And God shall wipe away all tears from their eyes, and there shall be no more death, neither sorrow nor crying; neither shall there be any more pain; for the former things are passed away.'

Q. Will heaven be their everlasting home?--A. Yes.

Q. And shall the righteous grow in knowledge and holiness and happiness for ever and ever?--A. Yes.

Q. To what place should we wish and strive to go, more than to all other places?--A. Heaven.

Pp. 93, 94: Q. Into what place are the wicked to be cast?--A. Into hell.

Q. Repeat, 'The wicked shall be turned.'--A. 'The wicked shall be turned into hell, and all the nations that forget God.'

Q. What kind of a place is hell?--A. A place of dreadful torments.

Q. What does it burn with?--A. Everlasting fire.

Q. Who are cast into hell besides wicked men?--A. The devil and his angels.

Q. What will the torments of hell make the wicked do?--A. Weep and wail, and gnash their teeth.

Q. What did the rich man beg for when he was tormented in the flame?--A. A drop of water to cool his tongue.

Q. Will the wicked have any good thing in hell? the least comfort? the least relief from torment?--A. No.

Q. Will they ever come out of hell?--A. No: never.

Q. Can any go from heaven to hell, or from hell to heaven?--A. No.

Q. What is fixed between heaven and hell?--A. A great gulf.

Q. What is the punishment of the wicked in hell called?--A. Everlasting punishment.

Q. Will this punishment make them better?--A. No.

Q. Repeat, 'It is a fearful thing.'--A. 'It is a fearful thing to fall into the hands of the living God.'

Q. What is God said to be to the wicked?--A. A consuming fire.

Q. What place should we strive to escape from above all others?--A. Hell."

The slaves are taught that they must do what God requires of them, if they would escape never-ending torments in hell. How strict an account of their stewardship does God require at their hands! He, they are taught, has made them slaves, and has given them nothing but labor and poverty for their lot in this life. Will he require much, where he has given little? Bishop Meade continues (Brooke's "Slavery," pp. 30, 31, 32):--

"Having thus shown you the chief duties you owe to your great Master in heaven, I now come to lay before you the duties you owe to your masters and mistresses here upon earth; and for this you have one general rule that you ought always to carry in your minds, and that is, to do all service for them as if you did it for God himself. Poor creatures! you little consider, when you are idle and neglectful of your masters' business, when you steal and waste and hurt any of their substance, when you are saucy and impudent, when you are telling them lies and deceiving them; or when you prove stubborn and sullen, and will not do the work you are set about without stripes and vexation; you do not consider, I say, that what faults you are guilty of towards your masters and mistresses are faults done against God himself, who hath set your masters and mistresses over you in his own stead, and expects that you will do for them just as you would do for him. And, pray, do not think that I want to deceive you, when I tell you that your masters and mistresses are God's overseers; and that, if you are faulty towards them, God himself will punish you severely for it in the next world, unless you repent of it, and strive to make amends by your faithfulness and diligence for the time to come; for God himself hath declared the same.

"Now, from this general rule,--namely, that you are to do all service for your masters and mistresses as if you did it for God himself,--there arise several other rules of duty towards your masters and mistresses, which I shall endeavor to lay out in order before you.

"And, in the first place, you are to be obedient and subject to your masters in all things.... And Christian ministers are commanded to 'exhort servants to be obedient unto their own masters, and to please them well in all things, not answering them again, or gain-saying.' You see how strictly God requires this of you, that whatever your masters and mistresses order you to do, you must set about it immediately, and faithfully perform it, without any disputing or grumbling, and take care to please them well in all things. And for your encouragement he tells you, that he will reward you for it in heaven; because, while you are honestly and faithfully doing your master's business here, you are serving your Lord and Master in heaven. You see also that you are not to take any exceptions to the behavior of your masters and mistresses, and that you are to be subject and obedient, not only to such as are good and gentle and mild towards you, but also to such as may be froward, peevish, and hard. For you are not at liberty to choose your own masters; but into whatever hands God hath been pleased to put you, you must do your duty, and God will reward you for it.

"2. You are not to be eye-servants. Now, eye-servants are such as will work hard, and seem mighty diligent, while they think anybody is taking notice of them; but, when their masters' and mistresses' backs are turned, they are idle, and neglect their business. I am afraid there are a great many such eye-servants among you, and that you do not consider how great a sin it is to be so, and how severely God will punish you for it. You may easily deceive your owners, and make them have an opinion of you that you do not deserve, and get the praise of men by it; but remember that you cannot deceive Almighty God, who sees your wickedness and deceit, and will punish you accordingly. For the rule is, that you must obey your masters in all things, and do the work they set you about with fear and trembling, in singleness of heart, as unto Christ; not with eye-service, as men-pleasers, but as the servants of Christ, doing the will of God from the heart; with good-will doing service as to the Lord, and not as to men. If, then, you would but say within yourselves, 'My master hath set me about this work, and his back is turned, so that I may loiter and idle if I please, for he does not see me; but there is my great Master in heaven, whose overseer my other master is,[I] and his eyes are always upon me and taking notice of me, and I cannot get anywhere out of his sight, nor be idle without his knowing it; and what will become of me, if I lose his good-will and make him angry with me?'--if, I say, you would once get the way of thinking and saying thus upon all occasions, you then would do what God commands you, and serve your masters with singleness of heart, that is, with honesty and sincerity, and do the work you are set about with fear and trembling, not for fear of your masters and mistresses upon earth, for you may easily cheat them, and make them believe you are doing their business when you do not, but with fear and trembling, lest God your heavenly Master, whom you cannot deceive, should call you to account, and punish you in the next world for your deceitfulness and eye-service in this.

"3. You are to be faithful and honest to your masters and mistresses, not purloining or wasting their goods or substance, but showing all good fidelity in all things.... Do not your masters, under God, provide for you? And how shall they be able to do this, to feed and to clothe you, unless you take honest care of every thing that belongs to them? Remember that God requires this of you; and, if you are not afraid of suffering for it here, you cannot escape the vengeance of Almighty God, who will judge between you and your masters, and make you pay severely in the next world for all the injustice you do them here. And though you could manage so cunningly as to escape the eyes and hands of man, yet think what a dreadful thing it is to fall into the hands of the living God, who is able to cast both soul and body into hell!

"4. You are to serve your masters with cheerfulness, reverence, and humility. You are to do your masters' service with good-will, doing it as the will of God from the heart, without any sauciness or answering again. How many of you do things quite otherwise, and, instead of going about your work with a good will and a good heart, dispute and grumble, give saucy answers, and behave in a surly manner! There is something so becoming and engaging in a modest, cheerful, good-natured behavior, that a little work done in that manner seems better done and gives far more satisfaction than a great deal more that must be done with fretting, vexation, and the lash always held over you. It also gains the good-will and love of those you belong to, and makes your own life pass with more ease and pleasure. Besides, you are to consider that this grumbling and ill-will does not affect your masters and mistresses only. They have ways and means in their hands of forcing you to do your work, whether you are willing or not. But your murmuring and grumbling is against God, who hath placed you in that service, who will punish you severely in the next world for despising his commands."

If the slave who wastes his master's goods and substance will not be able to escape the vengeance of Almighty God, what will become of the master who impoverishes and darkens the mind of his brother-man? Who commits the greater injustice,--the man who robs another of his mind, or the man who robs another of his money?

Mr. Glennie is equally explicit in his teaching. His fourth Sermon is on the text, Eph. vi. 7, "With good-will doing service, as to the Lord, and not to men," pp. 21, 22:--

"In this part of the word of God, servants are taught with what mind they ought to do their service. They are told to do what is required of them 'with good-will;' and to do it, 'as to the Lord, and not to men.'

"What a blessed book the Bible is, my brethren! It speaks comfort to all people in every station of life; it shows how every one must live here so as to please our heavenly Father. He, the Father of mercies and the God of all comfort, has in his word forgotten none of the children of men. All may learn from that holy book how their souls may be saved through the merits of the death of Christ. And, in addition to this, every one, in whatever condition he may be, will find in that holy book what his peculiar duties are. Thus, ministers are taught in the Bible how they ought to preach the gospel, and how they ought to live, so as to glorify their Saviour Jesus Christ. The rich are taught in the Bible how they must do good with their riches; and the poor, how they must be contented with the portion that God has given them; and both rich and poor are taught how to lay up treasure in heaven. Parents are told in the Bible how they must bring up their children in the nurture and admonition of the Lord; and children, how they must obey their parents. Masters are taught in the Bible how they must rule their servants, and servants how they must obey their masters. Truly, this holy word of God is a blessed gift indeed; and how greatly blessed shall we all be, if we diligently seek the help of the Holy Spirit, that we may be 'doers of the word, and not hearers only'! I will now read to you the whole of this passage out of God's holy word, which is written especially for your instruction:--'Servants, be obedient to them that are your masters according to the flesh, with fear and trembling, in singleness of your heart, as unto Christ; not with eye-service as men-pleasers, but as the servants of Christ, doing the will of God from the heart: with good-will doing service, as to the Lord, and not to men; knowing that whatsoever good thing any man doeth, the same shall he receive of the Lord, whether he be bond or free.' This passage from the Bible shows to you what God requires from you as servants; and there are many other passages which teach the same things. You should try and remember these parts of the Bible, that you may be able 'to do your duty in that state of life unto which it has pleased God to call you.' For, although a bad servant may not wish to know what God requires of him, yet a Christian servant will desire to know this, and to do his will in every thing."

How easy it must be for those who cannot read to learn from the holy book what God requires of them! Mr. Glennie assures his hearers, that not one of them will be able to say, in the day of judgment, "I had no way of hearing and learning about my God and Saviour"! (p. 137). May they not all listen to such words of comfort as fall from his lips? And how full of comfort to their souls must that book be which tells them that God intended to make them slaves, and that they must be faithful and obedient to their oppressors, if they wish to avoid endless punishment in hell!

Pp. 22, 23: "Our heavenly Father commands that you, who are servants, should 'be obedient to your masters according to the flesh;' that is, to your earthly master, the master that you serve here while in the body. Here is a very plain command: 'Servants, be obedient;' be obedient to your masters. A bad servant will not try and obey this command. A worldly-minded servant, who is not living in the fear of God, will neglect this command. But you, who call yourselves children of God, will do his will, and be obedient to your earthly master. You can every day give proof that you wish to serve God, by your ready, your cheerful obedience.

"You are here directed to be obedient to your master 'with fear and trembling;' that is, you ought to feel as anxious to discharge your duty faithfully as to feel afraid of giving offence by any conduct that looks like disobedience; for, by disobedience, you not only offend your earthly master, but you sin against God; and of this every Christian servant will be afraid. A bad servant will be afraid only of the punishment which he will receive, if his disobedience should be found out. But a Christian servant must look up always to his heavenly Master. Therefore, if you love God, whose children you were made at your baptism, you will do every day all that you have to do, with fear and trembling; that is, in the fear of God; knowing that he would be angry with you, if you neglected your duty. If you love the Lord Jesus Christ, who shed his blood for you, you will do your daily work with fear and trembling, lest, by any act of disobedience, you bring reproach on him whose name you bear. If you desire that the Holy Spirit should abide in your hearts, you will not willingly be disobedient, being afraid that this Comforter and Sanctifier would forsake you, if you paid so little attention to the plain word of God."

How full of comfort must the Bible be to the slaveholder! How gratifying to him the reconciliation between God and mammon! How interesting to a reverend father must be the reflection, that, just in the proportion as he serves his God, by imparting to his hearers gospel truth, he is serving mammon, and putting money in the purses of his employers, by making his hearers more valuable as slaves!

Page 23: "You are here commanded to be obedient, 'in singleness of your heart, as unto Christ:' that is, do not be double-minded, professing to be one thing, but really being another; but, in your duty to your master, have a single heart; an honest, upright, and true heart, as unto Christ; knowing that he sees your heart, and will not be pleased with double-dealing."

Page 24: "This part of the Bible goes on speaking of the same matter in different words; it gives 'line upon line and precept upon precept;' because it is what all of us ought to keep in mind, that we must engage in our several duties with a desire to please God, and with a fear of sinning against him. It says, 'not with eye-service as men-pleasers, but as the servants of Christ, doing the will of God from the heart.' Do not attend to your work, only when your earthly master's eye is upon you; but remember that the eye of your heavenly Master is always upon you. Do your work as serving Christ, look upon your daily tasks as the will of God, and do them from the heart, with a hearty desire to please God. A bad servant is an eye-servant, doing the work required of him so long as his master's eye is upon him: he has no regard to Christ our Saviour; and, instead of the will of God, he thinks only of his own will, and the desires of his own evil heart. But you, who profess to be the servants of Jesus Christ, will, if you are indeed his, do all your duty faithfully, whether the eye of man is upon you or not; you will feel that such is the will of God; and you will daily watch and pray, that, by the help of the Holy Spirit, you may 'do the will of God from the heart.'

"The word of God goes on teaching you the same thing. It says, 'with good-will doing service as to the Lord, and not to men.' A bad servant will very often do his service with a very bad will; he will try many ways to deceive his master, and will do as little for him as he can. You, however, who call yourselves the servants of Christ, will, if you indeed belong to him, aim at doing your service 'with good-will;' you will pray that your will may be subject to the will of God, so that you may 'do service' cheerfully, 'as to the Lord, and not to men.'"

We candidly confess, that we have not sufficient faith to believe that the Rev. Rector of All-Saints Parish would, if he were a slave, be a good servant, and do service as unto the Lord. We do verily believe, that both he and Bishop Meade would follow the desires of man's unregenerate and evil heart, and do their utmost to escape from this unwelcome service of Christ. But what a curious subject for reflection, that the saving of negro souls and of negro overseers in All-Saints Parish must keep pace one with another!

The Rector concludes his Sermon with these important suggestions:--

Page 25: "This passage of Scripture ends by telling you to remember that the day of judgment is coming, when every one, in every condition of life, shall receive according to what he has done in the body. It says, 'Knowing that whatsoever good thing any man doeth, the same shall he receive of the Lord, whether he be bond or free.' We are here told, that in the day of judgment, the inquiry will be, What have we done in this world? how did we live in this world? It matters not, we see, in what condition we have been here; it matters not whether we be bond-servants or freemen; it matters not whether we be among the high and the rich, or among the low and the poor, we shall in that day receive according as we now live. If we now live as obedient followers of our Lord and Saviour Jesus Christ, we shall, through him who loved us, inherit everlasting life. But if we are not true believers in him, if we are disobedient to his word, we can inherit only everlasting misery. With regard to you, the disobedient servants amongst you, the unfaithful, the deceitful, the ungodly servants, unless they repent and turn from the service of the devil to the service of God, shall surely 'be punished with everlasting destruction from the presence of the Lord, and from the glory of his power.' Whilst the obedient servants amongst you, the faithful, the true, the godly servants, who are living 'as the servants of Christ,' 'doing service as to the Lord, and not to men,' shall, if they continue steadfast unto the end, be blessed for ever."

We read in the Bible, that "God is no respecter of persons;" that "he hath made of one blood all the nations of men;" "Thou shalt love thy neighbor as thyself;" and that "all things whatsoever ye would that men should do to you, do ye even so to them." Would not the slaves be led to neglect of duty and insubordination by hearing such sentences? This effect, says Mr. Jones (speaking in reference to these sentences, "Rel. Inst." p. 197), "might result from imperfect and injudicious religious instruction.... But who will say that neglect of duty and insubordination are the legitimate effects of the gospel, purely and sincerely imparted to servants?" How judicious is the instruction given by Bishop Hedding! How purely and sincerely does Bishop Meade thus continue imparting the gospel! p. 116 (Brooke's "Slavery," &c. pp. 32, 33):--

"'All things whatsoever ye would that men should do unto you, do ye even so unto them;' that is, do by all mankind just as you would desire they should do by you, if you were in their place and they in yours.

"Now, to suit this rule to your particular circumstances, suppose you were masters and mistresses, and had servants under you, would you not desire that your servants should do their business faithfully and honestly, as well when your back was turned as while you were looking over them? Would you not expect, that they should take notice of what you said to them? that they should behave themselves with respect towards you and yours, and be as careful of every thing belonging to you as you would be yourselves? You are servants: do, therefore, as you would wish to be done by, and you will be both good servants to your masters and good servants to God, who requires this of you, and will reward you well for it, if you do it for the sake of conscience, in obedience to his commands."

From the same command of Christ, Mr. Jones instructs the slaves that they must not steal any of their own earnings, and must inform their masters when any of their fellow-slaves intend to steal! ("Catechism," pp. 114-116.) He never for an instant imagines (to use the words of the Rev. Dr. Jonathan Edwards in 1791), that "to hold any man in slavery is to be every day guilty of robbing him of his liberty, or of man-stealing" ("The Church as it is," p. 8). How solemnly would Bishop Freeman declare to the slaves, that thieves can never enter the kingdom of God, without thinking of the law of North Carolina, which provides that no slave shall be "permitted, on any pretence whatever, to raise any horses, cattle, hogs, or sheep" ("Rev. Stat." chap. 111, ?25), without the same being liable to be seized and sold, and the proceeds distributed, one half towards the support of the poor of the county, and the other half to the informer! (Ib. chap. 89, ?24.)

A friend once said that she was always grieved at receiving any expression of gratitude. She was grieved to think that the mere performance of duty was so uncommon as to call forth gratitude. In a somewhat similar manner, we feel more distinctly than ever how great is the degradation of the slaves, when such arguments as these can be addressed to them by intelligent men, with the expectation of producing conviction! How degraded must that slave be who does not feel or who cannot expose these wicked perversions of a beautiful command, and who cannot ask, in indignant tones, of these truly reverend fathers in God, "If you were the slave, would you consider yourself bound to work for your master faithfully?" Verily, "We owners and ministers" are "the almoners of Divine mercy" to the suffering slave!

Mr. Glennie declares, that God requires them patiently to submit to all the wrongs of slavery, as being afflictions sent by him for the good of their souls!--

Page 145: "Is it strange that any person who is loved by our Lord should endure sickness or pain or sorrow of any kind? No: this is what the whole Bible teaches. We read in one place, 'Whom the Lord loveth he chasteneth, and scourgeth every son whom he receiveth.' And in another place, 'As many as I love, I rebuke and chasten.' The Bible also tells us the reason of this, which is, that the children of God may be taught to repent more of their sins, and to be more submissive and obedient to God; ... that they may think less about this world, and may be more diligent in getting ready for heaven. For these good reasons, God chastises his people; and whenever you become sick, or are visited with sorrows, you should try and look up to God as chastising you for your sins, and should pray much to him for his Spirit, that you may be patient like our Saviour, when he suffered for our sins, that you may improve by his chastening, and grow more like him in holiness."--Pp. 128, 129: "Whenever, therefore, the sorrows of this life are pressing you sore, think of this saying of our Saviour, 'Every branch which beareth fruit, he purgeth it, that it may bring forth more fruit.' If you are indeed followers of Jesus, it will at such times comfort you to think that a Father's hand is upon you, chastising you,--in love chastising you to make you partakers of his holiness."

Mr. Glennie also frequently represents Christ as having appeared on earth as a servant, in order still more to reconcile his hearers to their lot (pp. 2, 3, 89). Nay, so anxious does he seem to be to induce his hearers to believe that Christ really endured the wrongs of a slave, that he sometimes goes beyond the Bible record. Thus, in describing Christ's sufferings before Pilate, he says (p. 9), "They spit in his face, and beat him with their hands; they scourged him, making long furrows in his back with the whip.... How grievous were the sufferings of our dear Lord!"

But he is not content with telling them they must patiently endure their wrongs: he also declares to them, that, unless they love those who wrong them, they are "going along the broad road that leads to hell"! He says (pp. 115, 116):--

"That we may all understand how the case stands with us, whether we are in the broad road leading to destruction, or in the narrow road leading to heaven, let us see what our Lord says about his sheep, and the mark by which they are known."--Page 117: "Our Lord says, 'By this shall all men know that ye are my disciples, if ye have love one to another.' Do ye hear his voice in this? Are you trying to love your neighbor as yourselves? Are you trying to do to others as you would have them do to you? Do you, for Jesus Christ's sake, love your enemies? Do you bless them that curse you, do good to them that hate you, and pray for them which despitefully use you and persecute you? In this way, again, you may try yourselves, and see whether you are the sheep of Jesus Christ."--Page 93: "If, in the great day, you would be placed on the right hand, you must, from love to Jesus, be kind to one another, and be ready to help any one as much as you can.... In your daily work, you should try and keep the Lord before you, and do it as to him, and not to man.... When any one offends you, you should, from love to Jesus, forgive him and pray for him."

Bishop Meade is equally explicit, pp. 131, 132 (Brooke's "Slavery," &c. pp. 33, 34). Senator Dickinson regrets that he was not born in a Slave State, so congenial is slavery to his soul! But the bishop, if he believes in his own argument, must be sorrowful that he is not himself a slave, so easy does he say is the slave's road to heaven!--

"Take care that you do not fret or murmur, grumble or repine at your condition; for this will not only make your life uneasy, but will greatly offend Almighty God. Consider that it is not yourselves, it is not the people that you belong to, it is not the men that have brought you to it, but it is the will of God, who hath, by his providence made you servants, because, no doubt, he knew that condition would be best for you in this world, and help you the better towards heaven, if you would but do your duty in it. So that any discontent at your not being free or rich or great, as you see some others, is quarrelling with your heavenly Master, and finding fault with God himself, who hath made you what you are, and hath promised you as large a share in the kingdom of heaven as the greatest man alive, if you will but behave yourself aright, and do the business he hath set you about in this world honestly and cheerfully. Riches and power have proved the ruin of many an unhappy soul, by drawing away the heart and affections from God, and fixing them on mean and sinful enjoyments; so that, when God, who knows our hearts better than we know them ourselves, sees that they would be hurtful to us, and therefore keeps them from us, it is the greatest mercy and kindness he could show us.

"You may perhaps fancy, that, if you had riches and freedom, you could do your duty to God and man with greater pleasure than you can now. But, pray, consider that, if you can but save your souls through the mercy of God, you will have spent your time to the best of purposes in this world; and he that at last can get to heaven has performed a noble journey, let the road be ever so rugged and difficult. Besides, you really have a great advantage over most white people, who have not only the care of their daily labor upon their hands, but the care of looking forward and providing necessaries for to-morrow and next day, and of clothing and bringing up their children, and of getting food and raiment for as many of you as belong to their families, which often puts them to great difficulties, and distracts their minds so as to break their rest, and take off their thoughts from the affairs of another world. Whereas you are quite eased from all these cares, and have nothing but your daily labor to look after, and, when that is done, take your needful rest. Neither is it necessary for you to think of laying up any thing against old age, as white people are obliged to do; for the laws of the country have provided, that you shall not be turned off when you are past labor, but shall be maintained, while you live, by those you belong to, whether you are able to work or not.[J] And these are great and real advantages, for which, if you consider things rightly, you cannot but thank Almighty God, who hath so wisely provided for your well-being here and your eternal happiness hereafter."

God has made some men slaves, in order the better to help them towards heaven! How admirably has the plan of the All-wise succeeded! The slaves are a nation of heathen in our very midst, daily and hourly (if we may believe their religious teachers) descending to everlasting perdition. From our very souls we are sick of the expression, "the providence of God," as thus cantingly used! Wherever a great wrong is committed by man, there the wrong is made part of God's mysterious providence! Are the poor oppressed,--it is a part of God's providence! Are bloody wars carried on for man's selfish ends,--they are part of God's providence! Nothing is too wicked, nothing too infamously mean, for that Being to do whose essence is love, whose law is just. We denounce the African slave-trader as a fiend, and, with appropriate religious ceremonies, hang him by the neck until he is dead, so deep is our detestation of a pirate; and yet, at the same time, we thank God, that, in his infinite wisdom, he has devised and executed the plan of negro-slavery, as the true way of Christianizing and elevating Africa! The slave-owner is said to have it in his power to shut up the kingdom of heaven against his slaves, and the power is said to have been exercised; and Mr. Jones seems to think that the race, taken as a whole, are thus shut out. And yet the slaves are called upon by right reverend bishops to fall on their knees, and devoutly thank God that he has made them slaves, in order the better to help them towards heaven! Truly wonderful is it, that ("Rel. Inst." p. 153) "they are living in manifold and gross sins; their iniquities are aggravated and great before the Lord, and not the least of them is their neglect and contempt of the spiritual mercies and privileges within their reach"!

We conclude our extracts from Bishop Meade's book with the following (Brooke's "Slavery," pp. 34, 35):--

"There is only one circumstance which may appear grievous, that I shall now take notice of, and that is correction.

"Now, when correction is given you, you either deserve it, or you do not deserve it. But whether you really deserve it or not, it is your duty, and Almighty God requires that you bear it patiently. You may perhaps think that this is hard doctrine; but, if you consider it right, you must needs think otherwise of it. Suppose, then, that you deserve correction, you cannot but say that it is just and right you should meet with it. Suppose you do not, or at least you do not deserve so much, or so severe a correction, for the fault you have committed, you perhaps have escaped a great many more, and are at last paid for all. Or suppose you are quite innocent of what is laid to your charge, and suffer wrongfully in that particular thing, is it not possible you may have done some other bad thing which was never discovered, and that Almighty God who saw you doing it would not let you escape without punishment one time or another? And ought you not, in such a case, to give glory to him, and be thankful that he would rather punish you in this life for your wickedness than destroy your souls for it in the next life? But, suppose even this was not the case (a case hardly to be imagined), and that you have by no means, known or unknown, deserved the correction you suffered, there is this great comfort in it, that, if you bear it patiently, and leave your cause in the hands of God, he will reward you for it in heaven, and the punishment you suffer unjustly here shall turn to your exceeding great glory hereafter."

Douglass's aunt Hester disobeyed God's commands, when she paid no heed to the orders of Capt. Anthony,--God's overseer. Accordingly, says Douglass ("Narrative," p. 7), who was an eye-witness of the transaction, the latter "took her into the kitchen, and stripped her from neck to waist, leaving her neck, shoulders, and back entirely naked. After crossing her hands, he tied them with a strong rope, and led her to a stool under a large hook in the joist, put in for the purpose. He made her get upon the stool, and tied her hands to the hook. She now stood fair for his infernal purpose. Her arms were stretched up at their full length, so that she stood upon the ends of her toes. He then said to her,--'Now, you d----d b----h! I'll learn you how to disobey my orders!' And, after rolling up his sleeves, he commenced to lay on the heavy cowskin; and soon the warm, red blood (amid heart-ending shrieks from her, and horrid oaths from him) came dripping to the floor."[K] Poor, ignorant, degraded aunt Hester! She little thought that God had ordered her not to visit her companion; and that, instead of shrieking, she ought rather to be giving glory to Him who was punishing her in this world, in order to save her soul in the next!

Bishop Ives thus instructs the slave-children under his charge[L] ("Catechism"):--

Page 27: "Q. You said that at your baptism you were made inheritors of the kingdom of heaven; but will you get eternal life in heaven, if you do not strive to go there?--A. No; but I shall be sent down to hell.

Q. How are you to strive or try to go to heaven?--A. I must have nothing to do with the devil and his works; which I gave up at my baptism.

Q. In what way are you to shun the devil and his works?--A. By keeping within me no bad thoughts; by speaking no bad words; and by doing no bad things.

Q. What do you mean by keeping within you no bad thoughts?--A. I mean that I must not hate anybody, nor wish to hurt anybody, nor wish to do any wrong.

Page 30: Q. What do you mean by doing no bad things, such things as the devil tempts you to do?--A. I mean that I must not hurt anybody; must not disobey my parents, nor disobey my master, nor disobey God.

Q. But can you not disobey your parents and your master without their knowing it?--A. Yes; but God knows it; for God always sees me.

Q. What else must you do to get to heaven?--A. I must believe all that God has told me about the way to get there.

Pp. 35, 36: Q. How are you to show that you love your neighbor as yourself?--A. I am to show it by always doing my duty to my neighbor, as God has commanded me.

Q. Who is your neighbor?--A. Everybody who lives with me and around me, and has the control over me.

Q. Can you name some persons?--A. My playfellows, my master and mistress, and my parents....

Q. How are you to show your love to your master and mistress and your parents?--A. I am never to lie to them, to steal from them, nor speak bad words about them, but always to do as they bid me.

Page 47: Q. How do others sin against you?--A. By cursing me, telling lies about me, or striking me.

Q. What must you do to those who thus sin against you?--A. I must forgive them.

Q. What if you do not forgive them?--A. Then God will not forgive me.

Q. Why?--A. Because I pray to him to forgive me, just as I forgive others.

Page 48: Q. How are you to forgive others, when they trespass against you?--A. I am not to hurt them, because they hurt me; but I must pray for them, and try to do them good.

Q. What if you do to them just as they do to you?--A. Then God will not forgive my sins, but will punish me.

Page 43: Q. What do you pray for, when you say in the Lord's prayer, 'Thy will be done'?--A. I pray that my will and everybody's will may submit to God's will.

Q. Where does God make his will known to us?--A. In his word and in his acts.

Page 44: Q. What are God's acts by which he makes his will known to us?--A. Every thing that happens to us is God's act.

Q. How are you to submit to God's will as made known in his acts?--A. When God sends trouble or sickness or death, I am to feel that God does right."

Mr. Jones thus catechizes the slaves ("Catechism," pp. 129-131):--

"Q. What command has God given to servants concerning obedience to their masters?--A. 'Servants, obey in all things your masters according to the flesh, not with eye-service as men-pleasers, but in singleness of heart, fearing God.'

Q. What does God mean by masters according to the flesh?--A. Masters in this world.

Q. What are servants to count their masters worthy of?--A. 'All honor.'

Q. How are they to do the service of their masters?--A. 'With good will, doing service as unto the Lord, and not unto men.'

Q. How are they to try to please their masters?--A. 'Please them well in all things, not answering again.'

Q. Is a servant who is an eye-servant to his earthly master an eye-servant to his heavenly Master?--A. Yes.

Q. Is it right in a servant, when commanded to do any thing, to be sullen and slow, and answer his master again?--A. No.

Q. If the servant professes to be a Christian, ought he not to be as a Christian servant, an example to all other servants of love and obedience to his master?--A. Yes.

Q. And, should his master be a Christian also, ought he not on that account specially to love and obey him?--A. Yes.

Q. But suppose the master is hard to please, and threatens and punishes more than he ought, what is the servant to do?--A. Do his best to please him.

Q. When the servant suffers wrongfully at the hands of his master, and, to please God, takes it patiently, will God reward him for it?--A. Yes.

Q. Is it right for the servant to run away, or is it right to harbor a runaway?--A. No.

Q. What did the Apostle Paul to Onesimus, who was a runaway? Did he harbor him, or send him back to his master?--A. He sent him back to his master with a letter.

Q. Is it any praise to a servant to be punished for his faults, or ought he to think hard of it?--A. No.

Q. Are servants at liberty to tell lies, and deceive their masters?--A. No.

Q. Are they at liberty to steal from their masters?--A. No.

Q. What ought they to show in their whole character and conduct?--A. 'All good fidelity, that they may adorn the doctrine of God our Saviour in all things.'

Q. If servants will faithfully do their duty and serve God in their stations as servants, will they be respected of men, and blessed and honored of God as well as others?--A. Yes.

Q. Will servants have to account to God for the manner in which they serve their masters on earth?--A. Yes."

Mr. Jones thus expounds the tenth commandment ("Catechism," pp. 118-120):-

"Q. How does God require me to love my neighbor?--A. As myself.

Q. Ought I not therefore to be glad when I see him have and enjoy every good thing?--A. Yes.

Q. But suppose I am not glad, and desire the very things he has, and begrudge his having them, what do I?--A. I covet.

Q. Is it not my duty to be contented with such things as I have, without coveting what my neighbor has?--A. Yes.

Q. What did the Apostle Paul say he had learned?--A. 'I have learned, in whatsoever state I am, therewith to be content.'

Q. Repeat, 'Godliness with contentment.'--A. 'Godliness with contentment is great gain; for we brought nothing into this world, and it is certain we can carry nothing out; and, having food and raiment, let us be therewith content.'

Q. From whom cometh down every good gift and every perfect gift?--A. From God.

Q. Who is exalted as head above all, and giveth riches and honor and greatness and strength, and also casteth down and maketh poor whom he pleaseth?--A. God.

Q. If I work and am industrious, and walk uprightly with God, will he suffer me to want any good thing?--A. No.

* * * * *

Q. Does this commandment forbid the very thought itself of evil against our neighbor?--A. Yes.

* * * * *

We are to be contented with our own condition and circumstances, as appointed unto us by our infinitely wise and gracious Father in heaven."

Thus discourseth that eminent son of Massachusetts, the Rev. Theodore Clapp, after seventeen years' experience of the blessedness of slavery (Sermon, p. 66):--

"Let all Christian teachers show our servants the importance of being submissive, obedient, industrious, honest, and faithful to the interests of their masters. Let their minds be filled with sweet anticipations of rest eternal beyond the grave. Let them be trained to direct their views to that fascinating and glorious futurity, where the sins, sorrows, and troubles of earth will be contemplated under the aspect of means indispensable to our everlasting progress in knowledge, virtue, and happiness. I would say to every slave in the United States, You should realize that a wise, kind, and merciful Providence has appointed for you your condition in life; and, all things considered, you could not be more eligibly situated. The burden of your care, toils, and responsibilities is much lighter than that which God has imposed on your master. The most enlightened philanthropists, with unlimited resources, could not place you in a situation more favorable to your present and everlasting welfare than that which you now occupy. You have your troubles. So have all. Remember how evanescent are the pleasures and joys of human life."

Judicious religious instruction, therefore, makes the slaves faithful, diligent, and honest, and very materially promotes discipline; and it produces these results much more perfectly than any other motive which can be used. The cowskin and the paddle are doubtless serviceable; but that South Carolina planter told the truth who said to Dr. Brisbane (Brooke's "Slavery," p. 35), that religion was worth more to him with his slaves than four wagon-loads of cowskins! A judiciously awakened conscience, an earnest wish on the part of the slave to do what he believes to be the will of God, in order to escape never-ending torments in hell, constitute a much more forcible and constant incitement and restraint than that of fear. When we reflect that "ignorance and superstition render them easy dupes to their teachers," and that the more ignorant and superstitious they are, the more easily they may be duped, it is evident that this religious restraint is easily created, and daily increases in strength. How infinitely more powerful, then, is such a motive than the fear of bodily suffering! It is equally easy and vastly more efficacious to ply judicious religious instruction than to ply the cowskin or the paddle!

It is evident also, that the religious instruction of slaves increases their market-value, and greatly promotes the safety of the community. "Experience teaches us," says the Right Rev. Dr. Gibson, "the great value of those servants who are truly religious, compared with those who have no sense of religion"

("Rel. Inst." p. 22). No persons feel this more sensibly than the slaveholders. "Even men of the world," says the Presbytery of Georgia, "throw wide the door of access to their negroes." The fourth of a series of resolutions reported to the Synod of South Carolina and Georgia in 1833 reads, "We deem religious instruction to master and servant every way conducive to our interests for this world and for that which is to come" (ib. p. 74). With the proceedings of a convention held in Charleston, S.C. in 1845, to consider the subject of the religious instruction of slaves, were published letters from several persons, describing the effect actually produced by such instruction. One person writes, "The deeper the piety of the slave, the more valuable is he in every sense of the word." Another says, "A regard to self-interest should lead every planter to give his people religious instruction." "On such large plantations," says Mr. Jones ("Rel. Inst." p. 239), "as a mere matter of gain, a religious instructor should be employed." By religious instruction (ib. p. 208), "the pecuniary interests of masters will be advanced as a necessary consequence."--Page 204: "Is it not conceded, that a truly pious servant gives less trouble, and is more profitable, than one who is not? Is there one master in a thousand who does not desire such servants? Is it not true, that the most pious servants exert the happiest influence in promoting honesty and good order on plantations and in communities?"--Page 210: "The religious instruction of the slaves will contribute to safety. 'The thing that hath been, it is that which may be;' and although, as a slaveholding country, we are so situated that, so far as man can see, the hope of success on the part of our laboring class, in any attempt at revolution, is forlorn; yet no enemy (if there be an enemy) should be despised, however weak, and no danger unprovided for, however apparently remote.... It is, then, but a prudent foresight, a dictate of benevolence and of wisdom, to originate, and set in operation, means that may act as a check upon, if not a perfect preventive, of evil. I am a firm believer in the efficacy of sound religious instruction as a means to the end desired."

Ib. p. 212: "Besides the general and special influences of the gospel now adverted to, safety will be connected with the very dispensation of it.... The presence of white instructors, settled ministers, or missionaries, in their private as well as public religious assemblies, and free intercourse with the people and with their influential men and leaders, exert a restraining influence upon any spirit of insubordination that may exist, and at the same time give opportunities for its detection. The negroes are as capable of strong personal attachments to their religious instructors as are any other people, and of their own will are inclined to make confidential communications"!

Such is the quality of the religious instruction imparted to slaves; such is the way in which their famishing souls are led away to the water of life! To escape everlasting torments in hell, a slave must submit to remain in slavery! He must neither murmur nor repine at his lot, but rather give thanks to God for his loving-kindness and tender mercy in removing from his path so many temptations to sin! He must obey his master in all things, and do the work assigned to him faithfully and diligently, "in singleness of heart, as unto Christ"! He must act honestly, and never waste any of "the comforts and conveniences of life" which he procures for his master. No accumulation of injuries or deprivations can excuse him for running away; but he is bound to endure all his wrongs with cheerfulness and patience, and, leaving his cause in the hands of God, look to Heaven alone for his reward! Who is there that does not feel irresistibly impelled, with Bishop Ives, to cease "wailing over the imaginary suffering" of the slaves, and to unite with him in "the heart-felt exclamation, 'How happy are the people that are in such a case! yea, blessed are the people who have the Lord for their God'"? (Bishop Ives's "Address to the Convention in his Diocese;" Jay's "Letter," p. 3). Who cannot say to the slaves, with Mr. Glennie (p. 58), "Your advantages are indeed great: ... oh! make full use of your privileges, and show that you thank God by serving him"?

To teach untruths is a greater wrong to a man's soul than merely to keep him in ignorance. How much more pitifully wicked is it, then, to teach such untruths only or mainly as must advance the pecuniary interest of the oppressor!

CHAPTER VI.

INDIRECT INSTRUCTION.--NO LEGAL MARRIAGE OF SLAVES.

"Marriage unites all which ennobles and beautifies life."--De Wette.

"Negro marriages are neither recognized nor protected by law."--Rev. C. C. Jones.

Besides the direct instruction thus imparted to slaves, there is an indirect instruction much more powerful and effective in securing their degradation.

"Marriage," says De Wette, "is genuine only when single and permanent. It is then also the first and most important institution of human existence; the foundation of all civilization and culture; the root of church and state. It is the most intimate covenant of heart formed among mankind; and thousands are first made aware by it that they have within them a nobler impulse and a nobler want than to labor, to acquire, and to enjoy. It is the union of manly strength with feminine gentleness; the tempering of masculine rudeness by female delicacy; and, for innumerable persons, the only relation in which they feel the true sentiments of humanity. It gives scope for every human virtue, since each of these is developed from the love and confidence which here predominate. It unites all which ennobles and beautifies life,--sympathy, kindness of will and deed, gratitude, devotion, and every delicate, intimate feeling. As the only asylum for true education, it is the first and last sanctuary of human culture. As husband and wife, through each other, become conscious of complete humanity, of every humane feeling and every humane virtue; so children, at their first awakening in the fond covenant of love between parents, both of whom are tenderly concerned for the same object, find an image of complete humanity, leagued in free love. The spirit of love, which prevails between them, acts with creative power upon the young mind, and awakens every germ of goodness within it. This invisible, uncalculated, and incalculable influence of parental life acts more upon the child than all the efforts of education by means of instruction, precept, and exhortation."

How true and yet how faint a picture of the vast influence for good of the institution of marriage! But if marriage thus unites all which it ennobles and beautifies life; if, as a means of education, its influence is uncalculated and incalculable, what must be the moral degradation of that people to whom marriage is denied? Must not the degradation also be uncalculated and incalculable? And yet such is the condition of the slaves! Not content with depriving them of all the higher and holier enjoyments of marriage, by degrading and darkening their souls, the slaveholders deny to their slaves even that slight alleviation to their misery which would result from their marriage-relations being protected.

It is obviously true, that (Jones's "Catechism," p. 112) "all the comfort and happiness of the marriage-state, and all the good flowing from it, to families and the world at large, depend upon its sacredness and purity." Without these there can be no marriage. No less true is it, that the institution ("Rel. Inst." p. 132) "depends, for its perpetuity, sacredness, and value, largely upon the protection given to it by the law of the land." But the law gives no protection whatever to the marriage of slaves!

"Slaves cannot marry," says the Civil Code of Louisiana (Art. 182), "without the consent of their masters; and their marriages do not produce any of the civil effects which result from such contract."

"With the consent of their masters, slaves may marry, and their moral power to agree to such a contract or connection as that of marriage cannot be doubted; but, whilst in a state of slavery, it cannot produce any civil effect, because slaves are deprived of all civil rights" (6 Martin's Rep. 550.)

"As the State," says a writer in the "Carolina Baptist," "constitutionally and legally is ignorant of the marriage of slaves, it is equally ignorant of its dissolution. It leaves this whole matter where it ought to be, that is, untouched, and with the owners themselves. If there be an abuse of this power, the remedy is not with the State, but social, religious, and ecclesiastical" ("The Church as it is," p. 77).

"Negro marriages," says Mr. Jones ("Rel. Inst." pp. 132, 133), "are neither recognized nor protected by law. The negroes receive no instruction on the nature, sacredness, and perpetuity of the institution: at any rate, they are far from being duly impressed with these things. They are not required to be married in any particular form, nor by any particular persons. Their ceremonies are performed by their own watchmen or teachers, by some white minister, or, as it frequently happens, not at all.... There is no special disgrace nor punishment visited upon those who criminally violate their marriage vows,[M] except what may be inflicted by owners, or, if the parties be members, by the church in the way of suspension and excommunication."-- Page 119: "The relation is liable to disruption in a variety of forms, for some of which there is no remedy."--Page 133: "Families are, and may be, divided for improper conduct on the part of either husband or wife, or by necessity, as in cases of the death of owners, division of estates, debt, sale, or removals; for they are subject to all the changes and vicissitudes of property. Such divisions are, however, carefully guarded against and prevented, as far as possible, by owners, on the score of interest, as well as of religion and humanity. Hence, as may well be imagined, the marriage-relation loses much of the sacredness and perpetuity of its character. It is a contract of convenience, profit, or pleasure, that may be entered into and dissolved at the will of the parties, and that without heinous sin."

What a pitiful and wicked mockery it is thus to expound to slaves the seventh commandment! (Jones's "Catechism," pp. 110, 111):

"Q. Should persons be married in a public or in a private way?--A. In a public way.

Q. And by whom should the ceremony be performed?--A. By a minister or some other lawful person.

Q. Is God really present to witness the marriage?--A. Yes.

Q. How near of kin may a man marry?--A. His first cousin.

Q. After marriage, can husband and wife separate whenever they please?--A. No.

Q. Has any person whatever power to separate them if he pleases?--A. No.

Q. What saith our Saviour, 'What, therefore, God hath joined'? A. 'What, therefore, God hath joined together, let not man put asunder.'

Q. Can husband and wife ever separate?--A. Yes.

Q. In how many ways?--A. In two only.

Q. What is the first?--A. When either of them commits adultery.

Q. What is the second?--A. When either of them dies.

Q. After one dies, may the other lawfully marry again?--A. Yes.

Page 112: Q. How will God punish those who break this commandment in the world to come?--A. In everlasting fire."

How sacred is the marriage of slaves! They cannot even go through the form, without the consent of their owners. And if the owner of two bodies consents to the performance of the ceremony "by a minister or some other lawful person," and God himself "is really present to witness the marriage," the law, notwithstanding, declares the so-called marriage to be as complete a nullity as the union of any other kind of live-stock! It declares that those whom God hath joined may be put asunder, whenever the owner pleases; as if, wishing to raise money to pay his debts, he finds it more convenient to sell the wife at auction to pledging his bank-stock; or if, wishing to remove, he thinks it will be better economy to take his stock with him than sell out, perhaps at a sacrifice, and buy again an inferior article! In order to be able to live with his wife at all, Henry Brown was obliged to hire her of her owner for fifty dollars a year; and, when her master became short of funds, he sold the wife and three children, before Brown's very face, to a Methodist minister,--one of those holy men who are "called of God" and "solemnly set apart" to preach to all men the gospel of love! So sacred is the marriage of slaves!

There is no such thing as a sacred marriage among slaves. Marriage, with them, at its best estate, is but concubinage. The relation must be entered into when and as the owner orders! It is changed whenever, in his good pleasure, he wills that it shall change! It ends when he wills that it shall end! Wherein is the union among the human stock, on the Southern plantations, regarded as more sacred and lasting than the union among the brute stock? In both cases, the law considers the union as a merely animal relation, for an animal purpose,--the increase, perhaps the improvement, of the breed! So sacred is the marriage of slaves!

The following advertisements, and hundreds of similar ones might be cited, throw light on the subject:--

From the "Richmond Enquirer," Feb. 20, 1838:

"STOP THE RUNAWAY!!!--$25 Reward. Ran away from the Eagle Tavern, a negro fellow, named Nat. He is no doubt attempting to follow his wife, who was lately sold to a speculator, named Redmond. The above reward will be paid by Mrs. Lucy M. Downman, of Sussex county, Va."

From the "Richmond (Va.) Compiler," Sept. 8, 1837:

"RAN AWAY FROM THE SUBSCRIBER--BEN. He ran off without any known cause, and I suppose he is aiming to go to his wife, who was carried from the neighborhood last winter. JOHN HUNT."

From the "Lexington (Ky.) Intelligencer," July 7, 1838:

"$160 REWARD.--Ran away from the subscribers, living in this city, on Saturday, 16th inst. a negro man, named Dick, about 37 years of age. It is highly probable said boy will make for New Orleans, as he has a wife living in that city, and he has been heard to say frequently that he was determined to go to New Orleans.

DRAKE & THOMPSON. "Lexington, June 17, 1838."

"$50 REWARD.--Ran away from the subscriber, his negro man, Pauladore, commonly called Paul. I understand Gen. R. Y. Hayne has purchased his wife and children from H. L. Pinckney, Esq. and has them now on his plantation at Goosecreek, where, no doubt, the fellow is frequently lurking. T. DAVIS."

The wife has been sold to the speculator in human flesh! The sacred relation has been for ever sundered by God's overseer! The husband has been orally taught to say,--"Thou shalt not commit adultery," and to consider such to be a divine command. But he is strong and healthy, and his master orders him to live with another woman. What is he to do? If he obeys, he commits adultery, and disobeys God's commands. Truly a difficult matter to settle!

What ardent prayers will the church send up to heaven, that their brother may have strength given to him to enable him to save his soul alive! What earnest entreaties! How solemnly will the church remonstrate with its member against the commission of so great a sin! And, when prayers, entreaties, remonstrances, have all been tried and have failed, how sternly will the church proceed to the last extremity,--excommunication! If the man who marries his deceased wife's sister must be cut off from "membership in the Saviour's body" as impure,[N] how much more must that man be cut off who is faithless during his wife's lifetime?

How admirably does the Savannah River Baptist Association harmonize the worship of God and mammon, and reconcile obedience to the commands of the master with obedience to God! This Association, in reply to the question (Brooke's "Slavery," p. 38),--

"Whether, in a case of involuntary separation, of such a character as to preclude all prospect of future intercourse, the parties ought to be allowed to marry again,"

Answer--

"That such separation among persons situated as our slaves are, is civilly a separation by death; and they believe, that, in the sight of God, it would be so viewed. To forbid second marriages in such cases would be to expose the parties, not only to stronger hardships and strong temptation, but to church-censure for acting in obedience to their masters, who cannot be expected to acquiesce in a regulation at variance with justice to the slaves, and to the spirit of that command which regulates marriage among Christians. The slaves are not free agents; and a dissolution by death is not more entirely without their consent, and beyond their control, than by such separation."

A similar decision was made by the Shiloh Baptist Association in Virginia. This question was presented for solution ("The Church as it is," pp. 76, 77),--

"Is a servant, whose husband or wife has been sold by his or her master into a distant country, to be permitted to marry again?"

The query was referred to a committee, who made the following report; which, after discussion, was adopted:--

"That, in view of the circumstances in which servants in this country are placed, the committee are unanimous in the opinion, that it is better to permit servants thus circumstanced to take another husband or wife."

Convenient truth! A different rule would lessen the productiveness of the master's stock! Can any man who owns the body of his sister be expected to acquiesce in a regulation which would deprive his property of half its value!

But, suppose the master wishes to sell the female slave for purposes of licentiousness, or suppose the master is himself impure, is this agreeable to the order of Divine Providence? Does any one say that either law or public opinion protects the female slave from the brutality of her master? The great frequency of outrages of this kind is demonstrated by the tens of thousands of slaves, more or less white, who are found at the South. It was a Southerner who said, that the best blood of Virginia flowed in the veins of her slaves!

From the "Richmond (Va.) Whig:"

"$100 REWARD will be given for the apprehension of my negro(?) Edmund Kenney. He has straight hair, and complexion so nearly white, that it is believed a stranger would suppose there was no African blood in him. He was with my boy Dick a short time since in Norfolk, and offered him for sale, and was apprehended, but escaped under pretence of being a white man!

"January 6, 1836. ANDERSON BOWLES."

From the "Republican Banner and Nashville Whig" of July 14, 1849:

"$200 REWARD--Ran away from the subscriber, on the 23d of June last, a bright mulatto woman, named Julia, about 25 years of age. She is of common size, nearly white, and very likely. She is a good seamstress, and can read a little. She may attempt to pass for white,--dresses fine. She took with her Anna, her child, 8 or 9 years old, and considerably darker than her mother.... She once belonged to a Mr. Helm, of Columbia, Tennessee.

"I will give a reward of $50 for said negro and child, if delivered to me or confined in any jail in this State, so I can get them; $100, if caught in any other Slave State, and confined in a jail so that I can get them; and $200, if caught in any Free State, and put in any good jail in Kentucky or Tennessee, so I can get them.

"Nashville, July 9, 1849. A. W. JOHNSON."

The following three advertisements are taken from Alabama papers:

"RAN AWAY FROM THE SUBSCRIBER, working on the plantation of Col.

H. Tinker, a bright mulatto boy, named Alfred. Alfred is about 18 years old, pretty well grown, has blue eyes, light flaxen hair, skin disposed to freckle. He will try to pass as free-born.

"Green County, Ala. S. G. STEWART."

"$100 REWARD.--Ran away from the subscriber, a bright mulatto man-slave, named Sam. Light sandy hair, blue eyes, ruddy complexion,--is so white as very easily to pass for a free white man. EDWIN PECK. "Mobile, April 22, 1837."

"RAN AWAY, on the 15th of May, from me, a negro woman, named Fanny. Said woman is 20 years old; is rather tall; can read and write, and so forge passes for herself. Carried away with her a pair of ear-rings,--a Bible with a red cover; is very pious. She prays a great deal, and was, as supposed, contented and happy. She is as white as most white women, with straight light hair, and blue eyes, and can pass herself for a white woman. I will give $500 for her apprehension and delivery to me. She is very intelligent.

JOHN BALCH. "Tuscaloosa, May 29, 1845."

From the "Newbern (N.C.) Spectator:"

"$50 REWARD will be given for the apprehension and delivery to me of the following slaves,--Samuel and Judy, his wife, with their four children, belonging to the estate of Sacker Dubberly, deceased.

"I will give $10 for the apprehension of William Dubberly, a slave belonging to the estate. William is about 19 years old, quite white, and would not readily be taken for a slave.

"March 13, 1837. JOHN J. LANE."

The next two advertisements we cut from the "New Orleans Picayune" of Sept. 2, 1846:

"$25 REWARD.--Ran away from the plantation of Madame Fergus Duplantier, on or about the 27th of June, 1846, a bright mulatto, named Ned, very stout built, about 5 feet 11 inches high, speaks English and French, about 35 years old, waddles in his walk. He may try to pass himself for a white man, as he is of a very clear color, and has sandy hair. The above reward will be paid to whoever will bring him to Madame Duplantier's plantation, Manchac, or lodge him in some jail where he can be conveniently obtained."

"$200 REWARD.--Ran away from the subscriber, last November, a white negro man, about 35 years old, height about 5 feet 8 or 10 inches, blue eyes, has a yellow woolly head, very fair skin, (particularly under his clothes).... Said negro man was raised in Columbia, S.C. and is well known by the name of Dick Frazier.... He was lately known to be working on the railroad in Alabama, near Moore's Turn Out, and passed as a white man, by the name of Jesse Teams. I will give the above reward for his delivery in any jail, so that I can get him; and I will give $500 for sufficient proof to convict, in open court, any man who carried him away.

"Barnwell Court House, S.C. J. D. ALLEN.

"P.S. Said man has a good-shaped foot and leg, and his foot is very small and hollow."

In the "New Orleans Bee" of June 22, 1831, P. Bahi advertises as a runaway "Maria, with a clear, white complexion." Ellen Craft is as white as our own sisters. Wm. W. Brown ("Narrative," p. 34), describing a gang of slaves who were under his charge, and destined to supply the New Orleans market, thus speaks of one who attracted the attention of the passengers and the crew:--

"It was a beautiful girl, apparently about twenty yeas of age, perfectly white, with straight, light hair, and blue eyes. But it was not the whiteness of her skin that created such a sensation among those who gazed upon her: it was her almost unparalleled beauty. She had been on the boat but a short time before the attention of all the passengers, including the ladies, had been called to her; and the common topic of conversation was about the beautiful slave-girl."

A friend, a resident for some time in New Orleans, describes to us a very beautiful slave he saw there, who had light curling hair, blue eyes, and almost a blonde complexion. After having been kept as a mistress by her owner, he finally sold her to pay his debts! No isolated case is exhibited by Wm. W.

Brown when he relates the history of poor Cynthia!

Is any sickly sentimentalist shocked at these recitals? Be of stout heart! Do not Christian bishops, and hundreds of other reverend fathers,--the messengers of God's everlasting truth to our souls,--assure us that slavery, "AS IT EXISTS," is right; and that, consequently, the fundamental maxim of slavery, "the child follows the condition of the mother," is right also! Why, then, should not the children of slave-women by white fathers be rightfully slaves? Of what consequence, then, is the pollution of the soul of the mother, compared with the fact of her increased value as a commodity? How utterly insignificant is the fact that a father holds his own children in slavery, compared with the advantages notoriously derived from such an improvement in the slave-stock? In sober, literal truth, the brother owns the body of his sister, and the sister that of her brother,--so sacred is the marriage-state of slaves! If the father wishes to repair the wrong he has done, the law forbids his teaching his own child to read or write! If he is poor, too poor to pay his debts, a creditor may seize his child in its very cradle, and sell it at auction to pay the debt! It ought not to be otherwise! Is it not agreeable to the order of Divine Providence, that a child should be sold to pay his father's debts? How fitting it is for Mr. Jones and Bishop Freeman to teach such a vendible commodity to say, "Thou shalt honor thy father and thy mother"!

Does any reader still doubt whether an owner thus has uncontrolled authority over the body of his female slave? Let him read the following extract from an opinion of the Supreme Court of the State of North Carolina,--the Old North State, whence Bishop Ives has long since ceased to weep over the "imaginary sufferings" of the slaves! To avoid a chastisement, a female slave ran off, and, on her refusal to stop when called, was shot at and wounded. Judge Ruffin, in delivering the opinion of the court (State vs. Mann, 2 Dev. Rep. 263), says:--

"The inquiry here is, whether a cruel and unreasonable battery on a slave by the hirer is indictable?... In criminal proceedings, and, indeed, in reference to all other persons but the general owner, the hirer and possessor of a slave, in relation to both rights and duties, is, for the time being, the owner....

"With slavery it is far otherwise. The end is the profit of the master, his security, and the public peace. The subject is one doomed in his own person, and in his posterity, to live without knowledge, and without capacity to make any thing his own, and to toil that others may reap the fruits.

"What moral considerations shall be addressed to such a being to convince him what it is impossible but that the most stupid must feel and know can never be true, that he is thus to labor upon a principle of natural duty, or for the sake of his own personal happiness? Such services can only be expected from one who has no will of his own, who surrenders his will in explicit obedience to that of another. Such obedience is the consequence only of uncontrolled authority over the body. There is nothing else which can operate to produce the effect. The power of the master must be absolute to render the submission of the slave perfect. I most freely confess my sense of the harshness of this proposition. I feel it as deeply as any man can. And, as a principle of moral right, every person in his retirement must repudiate it. But, in the actual condition of things, it must be so. There is no remedy. This discipline belongs to slavery."[O]

Judge Ruffin had not enjoyed the benefit of the instruction imparted some years later by Bishops Ives and Freeman. If he had, he would not thus have followed the dictate of a "desperately wicked" heart, and have repudiated the discipline of slavery as morally wrong!

The Rev. Robert J. Breckenridge, of the Presbyterian Church, himself a slaveholder, was a delegate to the State Emancipation Convention recently held in Kentucky. In a speech made by him before the Convention, he is reported to have said ("Louisville Examiner"), that--

"The system of slavery denies to a whole class of human beings the sacredness of marriage and of home, compelling them to live in a state of concubinage; for, in the eye of the law, no colored slave-man is the husband of any wife in particular, nor any slave-woman the wife of any husband in particular; no slave-man is the father of any children in particular, and no slave-child is the child of any parent in particular."

Who will venture even to conceive, much less compute, the deep degradation caused by the denial of marriage to the slaves?

CHAPTER VII.

"SOUL-DRIVING."

"A negro speculator, or a soul-driver as they are generally called among slaves."--Wm. W. Brown's Narrative, p. 39.

If we would most effectually degrade a man, we need only trample on the highest and holiest of all his rights,--his right to himself; we have only to make him the subject of barter and sale, a thing for speculators to make money on, for jockeys to deceive about, and for buyers to depreciate. And yet how few act as if they admitted this truth, or even faintly realized the enormity of this wrong!

Slaves, as subjects of property, are continually spoken of and treated as horses and cows, and other live-stock! Tens of thousands of advertisements might be adduced to prove this. We have room only for a very few proofs. The Civil Code of Louisiana provides:--

"Art. 2500. The latent defects of slaves and animals are divided into two classes,--vices of body and vices of character.

"Art. 2501. The vices of body are distinguished into absolute and relative....

"Art. 2502. The absolute vices of slaves are leprosy, madness, and epilepsy.

"Art 2503. The absolute vices of horses and mules are short wind, glanders, and founder."

In the "National Intelligencer" of May 2, 1843, the administrators of Alexius Boarman advertise for sale "twelve or thirteen likely young negroes, among whom are two carpenters; four head of horses, two yoke of oxen, several head of cows, all the sheep and hogs belonging to said deceased." The same paper of December 2, 1843, contains the following:--

"PUBLIC SALE OF VERY VALUABLE NEGROES AND STOCK.--The subscriber will offer at public sale at his residence, near Bladensburg, Prince George's County, Maryland, on Wednesday, the 20th of December next, if fair, if not, the next fair day thereafter, forty-five or fifty very valuable young negroes, consisting of men and women, boys, girls, and children.

"At the same time and place, he will offer his entire stock of blood horses, together with some farm stock.

"The terms of sale will be a credit of nine and eighteen months; the purchaser giving bond with approved security, bearing interest from the day of sale.

"Sale to commence at 10 o'clock, A. M. SAMUEL SPRIGG.

"The Marlborough Gazette will copy till day of sale."

In the same paper of January 25, 1843, directly under an advertisement for sale of "a girl about 18 years of age, who is honest, industrious, and a good cook, fine washer and ironer, and a good seamstress," we find the notice of a "Blooded colt at auction.--A thorough bred colt, two years old the coming spring, got by Farmer, dam by Lafayette"! D. H. Candler, the sheriff of Montgomery County, Md. in an advertisement now before us, states that he has seized on execution, and will sell "for cash only" at the Court House door in Rockville, "one stallion, Red Buck, and one negro boy, John"![P] To bring the case nearer home:--in the "New England Weekly Journal" of August 27, 1733, printed in Boston, we find the following advertisement:--

"SEVERAL LIKELY YOUNG NEGROES, best Barbadoes sugars, very good Bohea tea, bag Hollands, fine cambric muslins, and sundry other merchandise, to be sold by Hugh Hall, Esq."[Q]

In the "Boston Gazette" of October 21, 1734:--

"TO BE SOLD BY ----, Several likely young negroes, lately imported,--as men, women, boys. Also choice raisins of the sun, gunpowder, Newcastle glass, in crates and boxes."

Not only are slaves thus placed on the same level with other property, but they are treated in the same manner. As our horse-jockeys not infrequently color their horses, or put on false tails, for the sake of enhancing their value, so similar arts are practised by the slave-jockeys of the South! Wm. W. Brown thus describes a part of his duties, whilst hired to the slave-trader Walker ("Narrative," pp. 42, 43):

"In the course of eight or nine weeks, Mr. Walker had his cargo of human flesh made up. There was in this lot a number of old men and women, some of them with gray locks. We left St. Louis in the steamboat Carlton, Captain Swan, bound for New Orleans. On our way down, and before we reached Rodney, the place where we made our first stop, I had to prepare the old slaves for market. I was ordered to have the old men's whiskers shaved off, and the gray hairs plucked out, where they were not too numerous, in which case he had a preparation of blacking to color it, and with a blacking-brush we would put it on. This was new business to me, and was performed in a room where the passengers could not see us. These slaves were also taught how old they were by Mr. Walker; and, after going through the blacking process, they looked ten or fifteen years younger; and I am sure that some of those who purchased slaves of Mr. Walker were dreadfully cheated, especially in the ages of the slaves which they bought."--Pp. 45, 46: "The next day we proceeded to New Orleans, and put the gang in the same negro-pen which we occupied before. In a short time the planters came flocking to the pen to purchase slaves. Before the slaves were exhibited for sale, they were dressed and driven out into the yard. Some were set to dancing, some to jumping, some to singing, and some to playing cards. This was done to make them appear cheerful and happy. My business was to see that they were placed in those situations before the arrival of the purchasers, and I have often set them to dancing when their cheeks were wet with tears."

Can such treatment result in any thing but brutalizing every noble faculty? If advertisements of stallions and boys, blood-horses and men and women, blooded colts and young slave-girls, are considered so very similar as to be placed in the same paragraph, or alongside each other, how great a difference can there be in the treatment by the public of the two kinds of stock? Is the auction-block a scene for cultivating the affections of a poor slave-girl? Are the coarse and unfeeling jests there perpetrated calculated to increase her purity, or strengthen her moral sensibilities? Treat a man as you would have him to be, is a good maxim. Respect him, and he will respect himself. Continually disregard his holiest and best purposes, and in time he will do the same.

What but pecuniary profit does the speculator in horses look to? What other object has the speculator in men, women, and children, in view? Whatever mammon bids the slave-trader do, will be done. How much more than this, or will any thing more than this, be done? Will such a person consider as of any consequence the broken hearts of husbands and wives, of parents and children, who are torn by this terrible trade from all they hold dear in life, so long as their bodies are sound, strong, and healthy; so long as the investment retains its market-value? Of what consequence is deep, heart-felt agony to a speculator? Is he whose idol is gold to be turned from his purpose merely by the foolish wailing of a woman whose heart-strings are breaking? Do the cries of children made orphans, and of parents made childless, by his acts, move the heart of that man who makes his living by buying parents and children, husbands and wives, at the lowest prices, and by selling them, "singly or in lots to suit," to whomsoever will give the highest price?

The following is a well-known extract front an Address (p. 12) published by the Presbyterian Synod of Kentucky to the churches under their care, in 1835:--

"Brothers and sisters, parents and children, husbands and wives, are torn asunder, and permitted to see each other no more. These acts are daily occurring in the midst of us. The shrieks and the agony often witnessed on such occasions proclaim, with a trumpet-tongue, the iniquity of our system. There is not a neighborhood where these heart-rending scenes are not displayed. There is not a village or road that does not behold the sad procession of manacled outcasts, whose mournful countenances tell that they are exiled by force from all that their hearts hold dear."

In the "New Orleans Bulletin," we find the following "Slavery as it is," p. 168):--

"NEGROES FOR SALE.--A negro woman, 24 years of age, and has two children, one eight, and the other three years. Said negroes will be sold separately or together, as desired. The woman is a good seamstress. She will be sold low for cash, or exchanged for groceries. For terms apply to MAYHEW, BLISS, & CO. 1, Front Levee."

A similar advertisement will be found in the "New England Weekly Journal" (Boston), April 9, 1733; printers, S. Kneeland and T. Green:--

"A VERY LIKELY NEGRO WOMAN, that has a child of about six weeks old, to be sold, either with or without the child. Inquire of the printers hereof."

The following was a standing advertisement, a few years since, in the Charleston (S. C.) papers:--

"ONE HUNDRED AND TWENTY NEGROES FOR SALE.--The subscriber has just arrived from Petersburg, Virginia, with one hundred and twenty likely young negroes, of both sexes and every description, which he offers for sale on the most reasonable terms.

"The lot now on hand consists of plough-boys; several likely and well-qualified house-servants, of both sexes; several women with children; small girls, suitable for nurses; and several small boys, without their mothers. Planters and traders are earnestly requested to give the subscriber a call previously to making purchases elsewhere, as he is enabled, and will sell as cheap or cheaper than can be sold by any other person in the trade.

"Hamburg, S.C. Sept. 28, 1838. BENJAMIN DAVIS."

This is taken from the "Jackson (Tenn.) Telegraph," Sept. 14, 1838:--

"COMMITTED TO THE JAIL OF MADISON COUNTY, a negro woman, who calls her name Fanny, and says she belongs to Wm. Miller, of Mobile. She formerly belonged to John Givins, of this county, who now owns several of her children. DAVID SHROPSHIRE, Jailer."

How strong was that poor mother's love! She had toiled all the way from Mobile to the county where her children lived, and the laws of a Christian country consigned her to the jail! Perhaps, in her loneliness, she remembered some oral instruction like this (Jones's "Catechism," pp. 125,126):

"Q. Should mothers and fathers very tenderly love their children?--A. Yes.

Q. And, as they receive their children from the Lord, is it not their duty and privilege to present them unto the Lord in his own appointed ordinance, and to train them up for his church and service?--A. Yes....

Q. What should they teach them to do every night and morning?--A. Pray to God.

Q. What book should parents early make their children acquainted with, and out of which diligently instruct them?--A. The Holy Bible.

Q. Is it the duty of parents to pray with and for their children continually?--A. Yes.

* * * * *

Q. Is it their duty to warn their children of bad company, and keep them out of it?--A. Yes."

Poor slave-mother! very tenderly indeed did you love your children. But, in your agony, you forgot that it was wicked to run away,--even for the sake of teaching them to pray night and morning! How thankful, then, ought you to be to God, that, in his great mercy, he was willing to punish your transgression in this world, instead of the next!

We never so deeply feel the brutalizing effects of slavery as when we reflect upon its peculiarly degrading influences upon woman. On some accounts, we would gladly pass over this point in silence; but so atrocious a wrong should rest upon the heart of every one.

It is an established maxim of trade, that the supply eventually equals the demand. If the trade happens to be in men and women; in one way or another, men and women will be supplied to meet the demand. There is a great demand for slaves in the Southern and South-western States, because slave-labor is very profitable there. "The domestic cannot compete with the South-western demand for slaves," says a writer in the leading Democratic paper of Virginia ("Richmond Enquirer," Nov. 13, 1846). The slaves in the South and West do not increase fast enough to supply the demand. The foreign slave-trade is piracy. The only resource, therefore, which is left to those States is a domestic slave-trade with the Northern Slave States; where, to meet the demand, they resort to breeding slaves! Woman is degraded into a breeder!

Mr. Gholson, of Virginia, in his speech in the legislature of that State, Jan. 18,

1832 (see "Richmond Whig"), says:--

"It has always (perhaps erroneously) been considered by steady and old-fashioned people, that the owner of land had a reasonable right to its annual profits; the owner of orchards, to their annual fruits; the owner of brood mares, to their product; and the owner of female slaves, to their increase. We have not the fine-spun intelligence nor legal acumen to discover the technical distinctions drawn by gentlemen. The legal maxim of 'Partus sequitur ventrem' is coeval with the existence of the rights of property itself, and is founded in wisdom and justice. It is on the justice and inviolability of this maxim that the master foregoes the service of the female slave; has her nursed and attended during the period of her gestation, and raises the helpless and infant offspring. The value of the property justifies the expense; and I do not hesitate to say, that in its increase consists much of our wealth."

Hon. Thomas M. Randolph, of Virginia, formerly governor of that State, in his speech before the legislature in 1832, said:--

"It is a practice, and an increasing practice, in parts of Virginia, to rear slaves for market. How can an honorable mind, a patriot, and a lover of his country, bear to see this ancient dominion converted into one grand menagerie, where men are to be reared for market, like oxen for the shambles!"

President Dew, of William and Mary's College, speaking of the annual exportation of slaves from Virginia, says:--

"A full equivalent being thus left in the place of the slave, this emigration becomes an advantage to the State, and does not check the black population as much as at first view we might imagine; because it furnishes every inducement to the master to attend to the negroes, to encourage breeding, and to cause the greatest number possible to be raised," &c.

"Virginia is, in fact, a negro-raising State for other States."

Henry Clay, in his speech before the Colonization Society in 1829, says:--

"It is believed that nowhere in the farming portion of the United States would slave-labor be generally employed, if the proprietor were not tempted to raise slaves by the high price of the Southern market, which keeps it up in his own."

"It is a melancholy fact," says the same writer in the "Richmond (Va.) Enquirer," Nov. 13, 1846, "that negroes have become the only reliable staple of the tobacco-growing sections of Virginia, the only reliable means of liquidating debts foreign and domestic."

The following advertisement is taken from the "Charleston (S.C.) Mercury" ("Slavery as it is," p. 175):--

"NEGROES FOR SALE.--A girl, about twenty years of age (raised in Virginia), and her two female children, one four and the other two years old; is remarkable strong and healthy, never having had a day's sickness, with the exception of the small-pox, in her life. The children are fine and healthy. She is very prolific in her generating qualities, and affords a rare opportunity to any person who wishes to raise a family of strong and healthy servants for their own use.

"Any person wishing to purchase will please leave their address at the Mercury office."

Does any reader exclaim there must be some mistake; it is impossible that such a notice could be inserted in the leading political paper of South Carolina? Will he feel any more convinced by reading this, taken from the "Boston Evening Post" of September 10, 1744?--

"TO BE SOLD,--A likely negro wench, about 25 years of age, that can do all sorts of household work, especially cookery; is very hearty and strong; has proved her faculty at propagation, and is very fluent in the English language. Inquire of the printer."

Slavery is said to have existed in a mild form in Massachusetts! And yet we find in our own history parallels to some of the most brutal atrocities which can be perpetrated on any human being. So essentially the same is the character and effect of slavery, wherever it exists! Does any one, and who does not, feel deep disgust at these recitals? Let us rather feel disgusted at the system which leads to such atrocities! Let not our indignation rest upon the story of the wrong, but upon the wrong itself and its perpetrators.

Does any one say these are solitary instances of atrocity? Doubtless such advertisements are rare, but not unique. Others of the same kind, and still more atrocious, might be adduced. But which constitutes the greater atrocity,--to use men and women as "stallions" and "brood mares," or to speak or print the damning deed? If the latter shows hardened feeling, what does the former prove? If these advertisements were the only ones of the kind which could be cited, still they tell a story of brutal outrage, which is happening in this Christian land, every day, hour, and minute, to tens of thousands of human beings! Other advertisements, showing the brutality of the examinations to which women are frequently subjected, might be cited. But for these we must refer the reader to other anti-slavery documents; for enough of the disgusting details has been exhibited to establish our position.

To obtain any thing like an adequate conception of the brutalizing influence upon the slaves of this trading in their bodies and the bodies of their children, we must first see to what an extent it is carried. We shall confine our attention chiefly to those who make a business of the matter, "to gentlemen dealing in slaves;" leaving almost wholly unnoticed the vast number of instances of buying and selling slaves between private individuals, chaffering between neighbors, for their private ends! Not that this latter kind of slave-trade is any less degrading in its effects, but only because proofs in relation to the other are more accessible, and are amply sufficient for our purpose.

CHAPTER VIII.

"DOMESTIC SLAVE-TRADE."

"The traffic in slaves is irreconcilable with the principles of justice and humanity."--Treaty of Ghent.

No description of ours can give any adequate idea of the extent of this terrible trade. It is as regular a branch of business as any other that can be named. The city of Washington licenses persons to "traffic in slaves for profit"! The trade is carried on between Maryland, Virginia, North and South Carolina, Kentucky,--or the slave-raising States,--and Alabama, Mississippi, and the other slave-consuming States. Depots, or private jails, are erected at convenient places.

In the "American Beacon" (published at Norfolk, Va.), Jan. 24, 1848, appear the two following advertisements:--

"NEGRO REPOSITORY.--The undersigned has, at a very considerable expense, erected, and fitted up in a style of comfort and convenience, a commodious two-story building on Union-street, second door east of Church-street, for the safe keeping and accommodation of negroes, both male and female (the apartments being entirely separate), which are brought to this market for sale. This building is admirably adapted to the object proposed, having airy and pleasant rooms, and every convenience which could be desired, besides large yards, walled in high, a capacious cistern, &c. which, whilst they secure the comfort of the negro, likewise guarantee the most ample security for his safe keeping.

"In addition to boarding negroes for sale, the undersigned proposes keeping on hand from time to time, for sale, such negroes as may be in demand in this market, embracing every description of house and field-hands, male and female, young and old, that may be called for, and upon terms entirely accommodating.

"Besides the boarding and the selling of negroes, he will also make exchanges, giving or receiving such boot as the difference in age, character, qualifications, and appearance may notify.

"The highest cash market prices paid for negroes of both sexes at all times. WM. W. HALL."

"CASH FOR NEGROES.--I will pay the highest cash for likely young negroes of both sexes, from 10 to 30 years of age. All those that have such to dispose of would do well to give me a call before selling. I will also attend to shipping of negroes to any of the Southern ports, free of charge, when left with me; as I have a private jail for the safe keeping of servants. For further information, inquire at my office at Union Hotel, Union-street, or through the post-office. G. W. APPERSON."

The following is taken from a New Orleans paper:--

"SLAVE DEPOT.--J. Buddy.--Slave-yard and boarding-house, 159, Gravier-street, second door from Carondelet.

"House-servants and field-hands for sale at all times. Slaves will be received on board or sold on favorable terms. The building is a large three-story brick house, and very commodious as a slave depot. Particular attention will be paid to the health and cleanliness of all slaves placed in this yard."

From the "Missouri Republican," St. Louis, July 13, 1849:--

"REMOVAL.--Blakey & McAfee have removed to No. 93, Olive-street, six doors west of their old stand. They are prepared at all times to pay the highest prices for negroes. They have also a good secure yard, with a strong jail attached, and are prepared to board negroes sent to this market for sale. Persons having negroes for sale will please call and see us. Those wishing to purchase can find what they want at our yard. BLAKEY & MCAFEE, No. 93, Olive-street."

Hon. Horace Mann has described to us the slave-pen in the city of Washington; and another member of Congress informs us, that the United States jail in the District of Columbia is frequently used for the purpose of storing human beings for sale! Thus, in the "National Intelligencer" (Dec. 19, 1844), we find the following notice:--

"FOR SALE,--A likely young negro, in the jail of Washington. He is a most excellent teamster, and well acquainted with the care of horses. Persons wishing to purchase will apply to Mr. Ball, at the jail, where the boy may be seen, and further information given."

The activity of this trade may be inferred from these advertisements, which constitute but a small portion of what might be produced.

In the "National Intelligencer," March 28, 1836, three slave-traders in the District of Columbia advertise for twelve hundred negroes, and a fourth offers to buy any number! Here is one of the advertisements:--

"CASH FOR FIVE HUNDRED NEGROES, including both sexes, from ten to twenty-five years of age.--Persons having likely servants to dispose of will find it their interest to give us a call, as we will give higher prices in cash than any other purchaser who is now or may hereafter come into the market. FRANKLIN & AMFIELD, Alexandria."

In a later number of the same paper are the following:--

"CASH FOR NEGROES.--I will give cash and liberal prices for any number of young and likely negroes, from eight to forty years of age. Persons having negroes to dispose of will find it to their advantage to give me a call at my residence, on the corner of Seventh-street and Maryland Avenue, and opposite Mr. Williams's private jail. WILLIAM H. RICHARDS."

"CASH FOR NEGROES.--The subscriber wishes to purchase a number of negroes for the Louisiana and Mississippi market. Himself or an agent at all times can be found at his jail, on Seventh-street. WM. H. WILLIAMS."

In a later number, June 24, 1843, Mr. Richards is not so eager:--

"CASH FOR NEGROES.--The subscriber wishes to purchase twenty or thirty negroes, and will pay the highest market price. Persons having negroes to sell will find it to their interest to give him a call before they sell. I can be always found at my residence, corner of Seventh-street and Maryland Avenue. All communications through the post-office will be promptly attended to. WM. H. RICHARDS."

In a still later number, July 22, 1843, appears this:--

"CASH! CASH!--The subscriber wishes to purchase any number of negroes for the Southern markets. The subscriber will at all times give the highest market price in cash for likely negroes, mechanics and house servants included. Himself or agent can at all times be seen at the corner of Seventh-street and Maryland Avenue. All communications will receive prompt attention. THOMAS WILLIAMS."

The following are samples of some of the advertisements of Maryland traders. The original of all of these advertisements will be found at the Anti-Slavery office, Boston. We begin with one of Hope H. Slatter:--

"NEGROES WANTED.--Having returned from New Orleans, I will now pay the highest cash prices for all likely negroes that are slaves for life and good titles. All communications will be promptly attended to. HOPE H. SLATTER, Pratt-street.

"N.B. On the 7th day of June, 1844, Jonathan M. Wilson (my former agent), by mutual consent, withdrew from my employment, and is no longer my agent. HOPE H. SLATTER.

"Baltimore, July 29."

"CASH FOR FIVE HUNDRED NEGROES, at the old establishment of Slatter's, No. 244, Pratt-street, Baltimore, between Sharp and Howard-streets, where the highest prices are paid,--which is well known. We have large accommodations for negroes, and always buying. Being regular shippers to New Orleans, persons should bring their property where no commissions are paid, as the owners lose it. All communications attended to promptly by addressing H. F. SLATTER."

"NEGROES WANTED.--I have removed from my former residence, West Pratt-street, to my new establishment on Camden-street, immediately in the rear of the railroad depot, where I am permanently located. Persons bringing negroes by the cars will find it very convenient, as it is only a few yards from where the passengers get out. Those having negroes for sale will find it to their advantage to call and see me, as I am at all times paying the highest prices in cash. J. S. DONOVAN, Baltimore, Md."

"NEGROES WANTED.--O. C. & S. Y. Harris, of Upper Marlboro', wish to purchase any number of negroes, for which they will give the highest market price in cash. They will be in Port Tobacco once in every week. Any communications left in their absence with Mr. Lyne Shackelford will be promptly attended to."

"NEGROES WANTED.--The highest market prices will be given for negroes at all times. Persons having negroes for sale will please call at my office, No. 26, Conway-street, between Charles and Hanover. Communications promptly attended to.

"Also negroes will be received and kept at twenty-five cents per day. B. M. CAMPBELL.

"April 7, 1846."

"NEGROES WANTED.--Persons wishing to sell their negroes will find it to their advantage to give me a call before selling elsewhere. I have all the facilities that the trade will admit of in the New Orleans and other markets. Such being the case, I can give as much as any one else, which I am determined to do. Any communication addressed to me, either in Baltimore or Port Tobacco, will be attended to immediately. JOHN G. CAMPBELL, "Jan. 1, 1847. Agent for B. M. Campbell."

"TAKE NOTICE.--Persons wishing to dispose of their servants would do well to give me a call before they sell to the traders. By paying a small commission to an agent, they can get from $75 to $100 more; as I receive monthly from New Orleans, Savannah, Georgia, and Charleston, S.C. the full market prices for slaves. "SCOTT'S Intelligence Office, No. 10, Exchange Place."

The following is taken from the "Wilmington (Va.) Journal" of Sept. 3, 1847:--

"NEGROES WANTED.--I wish to purchase a large number of negroes, of both sexes, from the age of 14 to 30, for which I will pay the highest cash market price. As I intend making a long stay in Wilmington for that purpose, persons from the country would find it to their advantage to bring such slave-property to town as they have to dispose of. Also wanted some good carpenters, blacksmiths, coopers, and bricklayers.--Apply to me, at the Carolina Hotel. ANSLEY DAVIS, of Petersburg, Va. "Wilmington, May 7, 1847."

The following is extracted from an advertisement of Lewis A. Collier, a trader in Richmond, Va.:--

"NOTICE.--This is to inform my former acquaintances and the public generally, that I yet continue in the slave-trade, at Richmond, Virginia, and will at all times buy and give a fair market price for young negroes. Persons in this State, Maryland, or North Carolina, wishing to sell lots of negroes, are particularly requested to forward their wishes to me at this place. Persons wishing to purchase lots of negroes are requested to give me a call, as I keep constantly on hand at this place a great many for sale; and have at this time the use of one hundred young negroes, consisting of boys, young men, and girls. I will sell at all times at a small advance on cost, to suit purchasers. I have comfortable rooms, with a jail attached, for the reception of the negroes; and persons coming to this place to sell slaves can be accommodated, and every attention necessary will be given to have them well attended to; and, when it may be desired, the reception of the company of gentlemen dealing in slaves will conveniently and attentively be received. My situation is very healthy, and suitable for the business. LEWIS A. COLLIER."

The "St. Louis Daily Union" of August 26, 1847, contains the following:--

"ONE HUNDRED NEGROES WANTED.--The subscriber wishes to purchase one hundred negroes, of both sexes, for which I will pay the highest price, in cash. I can be found at all times at No. 104, Locust-street, by Gerard's stable. WM. JOHNSON."

"NEGROES WANTED.--For two hundred negroes, the highest prices will be paid by B. W. POWELL, City Hotel, or 51, Front-street."

The "Daily Reveille" (St. Louis), of the same date, contains the following:--

"WANTED to purchase, thirty or forty young negroes, by CURLE & GODDIN, 79, Olive-street."

The following is taken from the "St. Louis Republican:"

"NEGROES WANTED AND BOARDED.--The highest cash price paid for young likely negroes, at 104, Locust-street, between Third and Fourth, adjoining Gerard's stables.

"N.B. Our house will be well secured, and afford the advantages of a jail surrounded by walls, and a basement cell in it. WHITE & TOOLY."

The following two are found in the "Evening Mercury" of Jan. 14, 1848, published in New Orleans:--

"SLAVES WANTED.--Wanted to purchase, slaves of every description, at the New Orleans depot, No. 156, Common-street, for which liberal prices will be paid. Slaves will also be sold on commission, and purchasers are invited to call and see a well-selected lot of slaves offered at low prices. ELIHU CRESWELL."

"SLAVES WANTED.--E. Creswell, No. 163, Gravier-street, will pay the most liberal price for slaves of all descriptions; and those who have slaves for sale will do well to give him a call before selling to others. He will also exchange slaves, sell slaves on commission; and those who wish to purchase will do well to give him a call before buying elsewhere, as he keeps on hand a good selection of slaves, sold under full guarantee, and good reference for titles given."

The foregoing advertisements give us some faint idea of the demand for slaves. Those which follow are of slaves for sale. We cannot commence more appropriately than with these, taken from the "New Orleans Picayune:"--

"SLAVES FOR SALE.--Hope H. Slatter, who has retired from the trade, has sold to me his establishment in Baltimore, and leased for a number of years his old stand at the corner of Esplanade and Moreau-streets, at which place I shall keep up a large and general assortment of slaves for sale, imported direct from Maryland and Virginia. WALTER L. CAMPBELL, Successor to Hope H. Slatter."

"NEGROES, NEGROES.--Just received, and for sale at No. 7, Moreau-street, Third Municipality, a large and likely lot of negroes, consisting of field-hands, house-servants, and mechanics. Will be receiving new lots regularly from Virginia during the season. WM. F. TALBOTT."

The same paper of Oct. 18, 1846, contains the following two:--

"SLAVES FOR SALE, No. 165, Gravier-street.--The subscriber has always on hand a number of slaves, consisting of house-servants, field-hands, and mechanics, which will be sold low, for cash or negotiable paper. Persons desirous of purchasing will find it to their interest to call and examine. The subscriber will also receive and sell on consignment any negro that may be entrusted to his care.

"He would also respectfully notify persons engaged in the slave-trade, that he is prepared to board them and their slaves on the most reasonable terms. WM. H. MERRITT.

"Reference: J. Barelli, C. J. Mansoni."

"NEGROES FOR SALE.--We, the subscribers, have for sale, at our establishment, No. 159, Gravier-street (block in the rear of St. Charles Exchange), a large lot of valuable slaves, suitable for plantation, house-servants, &c. &c. Persons desirous of purchasing will find it to their interest to call and examine.

"We will also receive and sell on consignment any negroes that may be entrusted to us. We would also respectfully notify owners of negroes, and persons engaged in the slave-trade, that we are prepared to board negroes, and furnish traders with rooms, &c.

"Our house is roomy, airy, and dry. Terms reasonable. JOHN BUDDY. WM. H. MERRITT."

Mr. Wm. H. Bolton, whose name is appended to the next advertisement, is from Tennessee:--

"NEGROES FOR SALE.--I have again returned to this market, with eighteen or twenty likely negroes. I have located on the corner of Main and Adams-streets. I have plough-boys, men, women, and girls, and some very fancy ones. I intend to keep a constant supply through the season, and will not be undersold by any in market. My motto is, 'the swift penny; the slow shilling' I never get.

"I will also pay the highest cash price for young negroes.

"November 21, 1846. W. H. BOLTON."

To what uses these "very fancy" girls are put may be inferred from the following advertisement,[R] taken from the "Norfolk Herald:"--

"NOTICE.--For sale, a colored girl, of very superior qualifications, who is now in Mr. Hall's jail in Norfolk. She is what speculators call a fancy girl; a bright mulatto, fine figure, straight, black hair, and very black eyes; remarkably neat and cleanly in her dress and person. I venture to say, that there is not a better seamstress, cutter and fitter of ladies' and children's dresses in Norfolk, or elsewhere, or a more fanciful netter of bead bags, money-purses, &c.

"Any lady or gentleman in Norfolk or Portsmouth, who may wish to purchase a girl of this description (whom I consider the most valuable in Virginia), may take her and try her a month or more at my risk, and, if she does not suit and answer the description here given, may return her to Mr. Hill.

"The cause of offence for which I intend, though reluctantly, to sell her, is, that she has been recently induced by the persuasions of some colored persons to make her escape with them to the North, in which she failed, and is now for sale.--Apply to the subscriber, in Suffolk, or to James Murdaugh, Esq. or to C. C. Robinson, of Portsmouth, for further information. JOSEPH HOLLADAY."

Tennessee can also claim the honor of having such careful traders as Mr. J. S. Curtis:--

"ONE HUNDRED "A NO. 1" NEGROES.--I have on hand one hundred negroes, men, women, boys, and girls, at my depot, in Gaine's brick building, immediately back of Howard's Row, between the Gayoso and Herron House. I have judicious men purchasing in North Carolina, Kentucky, and Middle Tennessee, and will keep constantly on hand a large number.

"Persons wishing to purchase will do well not to trade, without first calling to see my stock. J. S. CURTIS.

"Memphis, November 20, 1846."

The "Spirit of Liberty" contains the following:--

"SOUTHERN PLANTERS, wishing to purchase negroes, would do well to give me a call before they make their purchases, as it would be greatly to their advantage. Negroes purchased and sold on reasonable commission. Apply at SCOTT'S Intelligence Office, No. 10, Exchange Place."

In the "Daily Richmond Enquirer," Sept 1, 1847, we find this:--

"NEGROES AT AUCTION.--On Monday, the 6th of September (Albemarle Court day), at Charlottesville, there will be sold at public auction about sixty valuable negroes, of every description.

"August 31."

In the same paper, Jan. 25, 1848, we find this:--

"TWENTY NEGROES.--Will be sold Friday, 28th inst. at 10 o'clock, twenty likely young negroes, viz. ten able-bodied men, three boys, four women, and three girls.

"Will be added to the above sale, a negro-man, 40 years of age, who is a first-rate carpenter by trade, also a rough blacksmith. "BENJ. DAVIS, Auctioneer, No. 3, Wall-street."

The following is taken from the "Alabama Argus," published at Dayton, Ala.:--

"FOR SALE SIXTY NEGROES.--By order of the Hon. the Orphans' Court of Marengo County, the undersigned, administrator of the estate of Moses W. Alexander, deceased, will, on Monday, the 5th of February, 1849, at the plantation of said Moses W. Alexander, deceased, in the Cane Brake, one mile south of Col. Pickens's mills, offer at public sale, to the highest bidder, a lot, numbering sixty, of the likeliest and best negroes ever sold in the South. They are all family negroes,--not bought up by speculators from every State in the South, but raised by different men, in families from five to twenty each. Among this stock of negroes are some able-bodied, stout, and valuable negro-men, and several likely young boys, from 10 to 18 years of age; also some likely negro-women, girls, and children. Among the same, A No. 1 cotton-pickers; a good weaver; and also one negro, who is a very good carpenter and blacksmith.--Terms of sale, twelve months' credit, with approved security. J.

M. ALEXANDER, Administrator. "January 5."

The following advertisement is before us ("Spirit of Liberty"):--

"VALUABLE SLAVES AT AUCTION.--I will sell on Saturday, the 14th inst. in front of the Market-house, one woman and her child. The woman is about 24 years old; and the child, a girl, about 5 years of age. The woman accustomed to house-business, also to the farm. The negroes are very likely, and warranted sound. They will be sold on a credit of sixty days for negotiable paper satisfactorily endorsed.

"Nov. 5. CHARLES PHELPS, Auctioneer."

The following is taken from a paper published at Opelousas (La.):--

"AUCTION SALE.--The undersigned will offer for sale, through the ministry of a public auctioneer, on her plantation, near Carancro, in the parish of St. Landry, on Monday the 5th day of February next, and the following days, one hundred choice slaves, of both sexes and different ages, among which is a good blacksmith and several other mechanics. These slaves will be sold separately, and under full and satisfactory guarantee of titles.--8 ox-carts, 69 work-oxen, 20 mules, 20 work-horses, 1,500 barrels of corn, 12,500 cypress pickets.

Conditions of Sale.--The slaves will be sold on a credit of one and two years from the day of sale; purchasers giving sufficient security to the satisfaction of the vendor, and the slaves remaining specially mortgaged until final payment of principal and the interest which may accrue thereon, at the rate of eight per cent per annum from time due until final payment. The conditions of the sale of the movable property will be made known on the day of sale. WIDOW HYPOLITE CRETIEN. "Opelousas, January 3d, 1849."

Literally speaking, tens of thousands of such advertisements as these might be adduced. You can hardly open a Southern paper without finding several.

Part of the trade is carried on by water. This part of the trade is regulated by Act of Congress (Act March 2, 1807, sect. 8-10), and slavers sail apparently with commendable regularity. The following notice is taken from the

"National Intelligencer" a few years since:--

"ALEXANDRIA AND NEW ORLEANS PACKETS.--Brig Tribune, Samuel C. Bush, master, will sail as above on the 1st January; brig Isaac Franklin, William Smith, master, on the 15th January; brig Uncas, Nathaniel Boush, master, on the 1st February. They will continue to leave this port on the 1st and 15th of each month, throughout the shipping season. Servants that are intended to be shipped will at any time be received for safe keeping at twenty-five cents a day. JOHN AMFIELD, Alexandria."

The two following advertisements are taken from the "American Beacon" of January 24, 1848, published at Norfolk, Virginia. They are advertisements of the same person, who, as we have just seen, offers to "attend to shipping of negroes to any of the Southern ports:"--

"FOR NEW ORLEANS.--Virginia and Louisiana Line Packets. The fast-sailing packet barque Bachelor, Page, master, will sail for the above port from the 20th to the 27th inst. For freight, cabin or steerage passage, for which she has good accommodations, apply to G. W. APPERSON."

"FOR NEW ORLEANS.--Virginia and Louisiana Line Packets will commence their regular trips to the above port the 20th September, and continue monthly throughout the season. They consist of the following vessels, to wit, barque Parthian, Capt. G. W. Allen; barque Bachelor, Capt. Hiram Horton; barque Phoenix, Capt. Nathaniel Boush.

"The above vessels are all of the first class, and commanded by long and experienced commanders.--For further information, apply to G. W. APPERSON."

This Capt. Nath. Boush is probably the same man who figures in Mr. Amfield's advertisement. But Southern traders by no means have a monopoly of this coastwise slave-trade. The barque Parthenon, Mellish, master, cleared from the port of New York, October 10, 1846, for Richmond, Virginia, avowedly "to load with slaves for the port of New Orleans."

How business-like is the following letter from a North Carolina slave-trader to his consignee in New Orleans! ("A Reproof of the American Church," p.

22):--

"HALIFAX, N.C. November 16, 1839.

"Dear Sir,--I have shipped in the brig Addison, prices as below:--No. 1, Caroline Ennis, $650; 2, Silvy Holland, $625; 3, Silvy Booth, $487.50; 4, Maria Pollock, $475; 5, Emeline Pollock, $475; 6, Delia Averit, $475.

"The two girls that cost $650 and $625 were bought before I shipped my first. I have a great many negroes offered to me; but I will not pay the prices they ask, for I know they will come down. I have no opposition in market. I will wait until I hear from you before I buy, and then I can judge what I must pay. Goodwin will send you the bill of lading for my negroes, as he shipped them with his own. Write often, as the times are critical, and it depends on the prices you get to govern me in buying. "Yours, &c. G. W. BARNES. "Mr. Theophilus Freeman, New Orleans."

The number of slaves thus bought and sold can never be known with perfect accuracy. Hon. John G. Palfrey, in his excellent Papers on the Slave Power (p. 83), estimates the number annually sold from the more northerly Slave States at not less than forty thousand! We think his estimate within the truth.

In the course of a single year, 1835-6, no less than forty thousand slaves are said to have been sold out of Virginia alone! ("Niles's Reg." Oct. 8, 1836.) The "New York Journal of Commerce" of Oct. 12, 1835, contained a letter from a Virginian, whom the editor calls "a very good and sensible man," asserting that twenty thousand slaves had been driven to the South from Virginia during that year, of which nearly one fourth was then remaining. But 1835 and 1836 were years of great speculation. In 1837 the consequent severe pressure in the money market was attributed by a committee of the citizens of Mobile (Ala.) in part to over-trading in slaves. Their report states, that purchases by Alabama of that species of property from other States since 1833 have amounted to about ten million dollars annually.

The slaves increase in about the same ratio in all of the Slave States. If the warmer latitudes of the extreme South are more congenial to them, and favor their increase more than the climate of Virginia, this effect is, at least, fully balanced by the great amount and unhealthy character of much of the labor on the sugar, rice, and cotton plantations, and by the great extent to which slave-breeding is carried in the more northern States. The following table exhibits the rates of increase of the slaves, every ten years, from 1790 to 1840:--

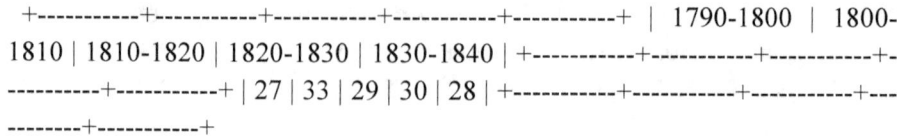

1790-1800	1800-1810	1810-1820	1820-1830	1830-1840
27	33	29	30	28

Accordingly, for the fifty years ending in 1840, the slaves increased on an average a little over twenty-eight per cent every ten years. We adopt this as a fair statement of what should be their decennial natural increase in all the States; and, by natural increase, we mean increase from births. The following tables explain themselves:--

SLAVE-EXPORTING STATES.

Name of State.	Slaves in each State in 1830.	Slaves in 1840.	Number which ought to have been in 1840.	Decrease every ten years.	Annual decrease.
Delaware	3,292	2,605	4,214	1,619	162
Maryland	102,294	89,737	130,936	41,199	4,120
Dis. of Columbia	6,119	4,694	7,833	3,139	313
Virginia	469,757	448,987	601,289	152,302	15,230
North Carolina	235,601	245,817	301,569	55,752	5,575
South Carolina	315,401	327,038	403,713	76,675	7,668
Kentucky	165,213	182,258	211,473	29,215	2,922
Tennessee	681,904	829,210	872,837	43,627	4,363
Total		2130,346		403,528	40,353

SLAVE-IMPORTING STATES.

Name of State.	Slaves in each State in 1830.	Slaves in 1840.	Number which ought to have been in 1840.	Extra decennial increase.	Extra annual increase.
Georgia	217,531	280,944	278,440	2,504	250
Florida	15,501	25,717	19,841	5,876	587
Alabama	117,549	253,532	150,462	103,070	10,307
Mississippi	65,659	195,211	84,043	111,168	11,117
Louisiana	109,588	168,452	140,273	28,179	2,818
Arkansas	4,576	19,935	5,857	14,078	1,408

Missouri	25,081	58,240	32,104	26,136	2,614
Total				291,011	29,101

The census of 1840, therefore, exhibits an annual unnatural decrease of over forty thousand of the slave-population in the exporting States. But this census, at least so far as statistics touching slaves and free colored persons are concerned, is notoriously and grossly incorrect. Either it or the tables prepared from it in the State Department have been dishonestly prepared, or very much garbled, apparently with the intent to prove that slavery was better calculated to secure the health of the negro race than a state of freedom. What figures will tell in favor of slavery?--not, what figures will tell the truth?--seems to have been the principle on which the last census was taken. Such being the case, we feel confident that the census makes the slaves in the exporting States decrease as little as possible. In 1830, Virginia had 469,757 slaves. In 1840 she ought to have had this number, and their natural increase for ten years, 135,532. Instead of this, all the natural increase is gone, and 20,770 besides! All will see that such a statement would tell too strongly against slavery to be admitted into a census got up under such slave-supporting auspices, unless the statement was really within the truth.

We believe, therefore, that the census of 1850, if truly taken, will exhibit a much larger annual unnatural decrease of the slave-population in the exporting States. This decrease, whatever it may really be, has not been owing to manumissions. It has not been caused by slaves running away. For the effects of both these causes, the surplus over 40,000 would be a liberal allowance. This unnatural decrease must, then, be caused by the slave-trade, and the migration of planters with their slaves. The fact is beyond all question, that every year forty thousand men, women, and children are torn from their homes and friends, and driven to the South and West. So truly did the Rev. Theodore Clapp speak (Sermon, p. 46), when he declared, "Slaves possess the inappreciable benefits which grow out of the endearing ties of friendship, kindred, sympathy, and the whole class of domestic affections. Parents and children, husbands and wives (it is true), are sometimes separated by being involved in those calamities which sweep away the possessions and prosperity of the master. But, take it all in all, they are as free and undisturbed in the enjoyment of their domestic relations, as the white inhabitants of the Northern States"! Forty thousand fathers, mothers, brothers, sisters, and children are every year carried from the places of their birth, like so many cattle, although the terrible fact is well known that at least one fourth of them must die in the process of acclimation![S] So very tender is man of man, when he holds his brother in slavery, and makes merchandise of his sister! So eager is the soul-driver to coin his brother's blood into dollars! So ready are those whom "God has appointed masters" to sacrifice the lives of one fourth of those committed to their charge, in order greatly to advance the market value of the survivors!

We have no data from which to infer the number of planters who go South with their slaves. But, allowing that five hundred thus remove, and that on an average they have ten slaves each (proper estimates we believe), we have left thirty-five thousand as the number of human beings who are every year sold to the speculators in human flesh!

Now, Mr. Barnes's "lot" of his fellow-creatures averaged in value over five hundred dollars apiece; and those were times when, from his account, the market was glutted, and the prices accordingly low. "Young and likely" negroes are more easily acclimated, and are better able to work, than others. Consequently, they are the ones most sought after by judicious traders. We should consider five hundred dollars for a young, healthy negro, warranted sound, as really a low price. But, if we suppose the slaves annually exported to be worth less than any of Mr. Barnes's lot,--considering them as worth only $450 apiece,--we have, as the sums of money every year invested in the trade in slaves, the very moderate sum of fifteen millions seven hundred and fifty thousand dollars! This is exclusive of the cost of all the private jails, of transportation by sea and land, food, wages of drivers, &c.; which cannot but very largely increase this sum. This sum, $15,750,000, would, in less than three years, double the number of miles of railroad which were in operation in all the Southern States in 1846 (Parker's "Letter on Slavery," p. 52). It would, in only two years, more than double in length all the railroads which were then in operation in all the Slave States, except Maryland. It costs every year five millions more to carry on the domestic slave-trade than it does to fit out and victual all the whale-ships of the United States! ("American Almanac, 1843," p. 178.) Over one fifth of the entire value of the cotton, sugar, rice, and tobacco raised in the fifteen Slave States in 1839, and over one third of the value of articles manufactured in the South, was invested in slaves! Nearly twice as many slaves are carried South and West every year as there are men in all the Slave States engaged in the learned professions!--so terribly prominent is this trade in men and women! Who will venture to conceive, much less express, the deep degradation which must be caused by a trade of such fearful character and magnitude;--degradation not only to the immediate sufferers, but to all those who may be subjected to it?

CHAPTER IX.

RUNAWAY SLAVES.

"It is contrary also to the will of God for servants either to run away, or harbor a runaway"--Rev. C. C. Jones's Teaching to Slaves.

The treatment which runaway slaves receive cannot but greatly degrade them. Pious as well as worldly masters consider that their slaves have no more right to run away than their horses or mules. The Christian slaveholder orally teaches his slaves, that, by taking this step, they sin in the sight of God; for has not Paul most emphatically condemned the practice? So careful is he of the souls of those whom God has committed to his charge!

We frequently find advertisements similar to this, cut from the "American Beacon" (Norfolk, Va.), Jan. 24, 1848:--

"$50 REWARD.--Stop Ruffin and Wyatt.--These men left my house on Saturday night, January 15, 1848, without any provocation. They have uniformly maintained a good character for honesty, industry, and sobriety,-- were obedient and trustworthy servants, and no severity nor threats had been offered towards them; and I very much fear they have left for some Northern State.

* * * * *

"These slaves were originally owned in Surry, and possibly may be in the vicinity of their relatives. GEORGE N. HATCH.

"Gaysville, P.O. Prince George County, Va."

Good Mr. Bryant Johnson is very much more indignant. In the "Macon (Georgia) Telegraph," May 28, is the following:--

"About the first of March last, the negro-man, Ransom, left me without the least provocation whatever. I will give a reward of $20 for said negro if taken, dead or alive; and, if killed in any attempt, an advance of $5 will be paid. BRYANT JOHNSON.

"Crawford County, Georgia."

In the extremity of his wrath, he cannot think of the least provocation whatever which he has given his slave. But we confess we are much more touched by friend Hatch's advertisement. Simple-minded creature! He evidently speaks more in sorrow and astonishment than in anger. Doubtless he had uniformly fed, clothed, and housed his servants well, and had never been severe with or threatened them. How could they desire to leave him? They have run away without any provocation! So unnatural, almost impossible, in the eyes of masters, is any spark of manliness in a slave! They cannot conceive it possible for a manly love of liberty to provoke a favored negro to run away. Still, however, even favored servants are continually escaping from their happy state; and, by the methods adopted to retake them, they are most efficiently taught that they have no more rights than has a favored hound or a valued horse. Their manliness is crushed, until at last they really feel themselves to be little else than items of profit or loss to their owners. The old slave who, at the point of death, was asked whether he was not sorry to die, and who replied, "Oh! no: the loss is massa's," had very faithfully improved the instruction imparted to his class.

If our horse is stolen from his stable, or our cow strays from her pasture, we advertise them as "strayed or stolen." If a slave runs away, his master advertises him, and offers a reward for his capture. If he is found, the lucky finder deposits him in jail for safe keeping, to await a favorable opportunity of sending him back to his master,--of course, like Onesimus, as a brother beloved. The jailer gets his legal fees, the finder gets his reward, the master gets his slave, and the slave most generally receives some "moderate correction" from the cowskin or the paddle. If he will not listen to the teaching of God's messengers to his soul, who are continually repeating to him (Jones's "Rel. Inst." 188) "a servant who knows his master's duty, and will not do it, must be made to do it," how can he complain of his treatment?

So anxious are they at the South that every poor African should have a good, kind master to attend to the wants of his soul, and support him in old age, that, if a stray negro is taken up running at large without an apparent owner, and for any cause he cannot legally prove his freedom, even though he does really own himself, he is nevertheless advertised, and sold at auction to the highest bidder, to pay the expenses occasioned by his own capture and detention. How happy must be the people that are in such a case! Yea, blessed is his condition whose body is fed and whipped, whose soul is saved and darkened, by his brother man!

The "Revised Statutes" of NORTH CAROLINA, chap. 111, sec. 11, provides that,--

"If any negro who shall be taken up as a runaway, and brought before any justice of the peace, will not declare the name of his or her owner, such justice shall in such case, and he is hereby required, by a warrant under his hand, to commit the said negro-slave to the jail of the county wherein he or she shall be taken up; and the sheriff or undersheriff of the county into whose custody the said runaway shall be committed, shall forthwith cause notice in writing of such commitment to be set up on the Court-house door of the said county, and there continued during the space of two months; in which notice a full description of the said runaway and his clothing shall be particularly set down."--When the owner is supposed to be a resident in another State, the jailer is obliged by sec. 15, "by the first opportunity after such commitment, to send a description of such negro or runaway, together with the account of the time of commitment, and the county where such runaway is committed, to the press, to be advertised in the State Gazette."--Sec. 16 provides, that, "whenever any negro-slave shall be taken up in this State as a runaway, and confined in any jail for the space of twelve months, and the apprehension and confinement of said slave have been advertised in the State Gazette at least six months, and the owner does not apply to prove property in said time, then it shall be lawful for the court of pleas and quarter sessions of the county in which said runaway is confined, to command their sheriff to expose said negro-slave to public sale for ready money, giving three months' notice in some public newspaper in this State, at the Court-house door, and at two other public places in the said county, of the time and place of sale, and of the circumstances under which the said slave is to be sold."--Sect. 17 gives the sheriff "two and a half per centum on the amount of sale."--Sect. 18 declares that "the bill of sale of the sheriff shall vest in the purchaser an absolute right to the said slave." The residue of the amount of sales, after deducting commissions and prison charges, is directed to be paid to the county trustee for the use of the county.

Similar laws, authorizing the sale into slavery of negroes taken up as runaway slaves, who cannot from any cause prove their freedom, are found in Virginia, South Carolina, Georgia, Kentucky, Tennessee, Florida, Alabama, Mississippi, Missouri, Arkansas, and Louisiana. A similar law has always existed in the District of Columbia, originally enacted, and since supported, by Northern freemen. Our law, however, differs from the others in offering to the marshal a high bribe to induce him to sell free negroes, by providing that the proceeds of the persons sold may remain in his own pocket, unless after the sale the master shall be discovered, and shall claim the balance.

Throughout all the Slave States, the law presumes every free negro to be a slave, until he can legally prove his freedom. Consequently, every free negro, out of his own neighborhood, is presumed to be, and treated as, a runaway slave, until he can establish his freedom. Under laws of this kind, many free negroes are taken; and, if from want of money or friends, or distance from home, or any other cause, they cannot prove their freedom, as no owner can come forward and "claim property and pay charges," they must necessarily be sold into slavery for life!

Very recently, in the columns of the "Washington Union," appeared the following notices:--

"NOTICE.--Was committed to the jail of Washington County, D.C. on the 5th July, 1846, as a runaway, a negro-man, who calls himself John Crew. He is black, about 5 feet 6-1/2 inches high, and about 43 years of age. He says he is free, and was born in Hanover County, Virginia, and was set free by Mrs. Allen, formerly Mrs. Watson, of said county; and that he lived with Jude & Muir, in Richmond, Virginia; and that he obtained his free papers in Richmond in 1823, when a Mr. Henning was clerk of the court. He has had right leg broken, which has left a large scar on it. He has a scar on the right side of his neck, which he says he has received since he left Richmond.

"The owner or owners of the above-described negro-man are hereby required to come forward, prove him, and take him away, or he will be sold for his prison and other expenses, as the law directs. ROBT. BALL, Jailer for "Aug. 15. A. HUNTER, Marshal."

"NOTICE.--Was committed to the jail of Washington County, D.C. on the 23d of July, 1847, as a runaway, a negro-woman, who calls herself Ann E. Hodges. She is nearly black, about 5 feet 5-1/4 inches high, and about 22 years of age. Had on, when committed, a slate-colored Merino dress and a brown calico sun-bonnet. She says she is free, and served her time out with a Mr. Benjamin Daltry, of Southampton, Va.; and that Messrs. Griffin & Bishop, of the same place, know her to be free. She has two scars on the left leg, near the knee, from the bite of a dog, one on her left wrist, and one on the point of her breast-bone, occasioned by a burn.

"The owner or owners of the above-described negro-woman are hereby required to come forward, prove her, and take her away, or she will be sold for her prison and other expenses, as the law directs. ROBT. BALL, Jailer, for "Aug. 23. A. HUNTER, Marshal."

Here is another instance, which happened several years since:--

"NOTICE.--Was committed to the jail of Washington County, District of Columbia, as a runaway, a negro-woman, by the name of Polly Leiper, and her infant child, William.... Says she was set free by John Campbell, of Richmond, Va. in 1818 or 1819. The owner of the above-described woman and child, if any, are requested to come and prove them, and take them away, or they will be sold for their jail fees and other expenses, as the law directs. TENCH RINGGOLD, Marshal. "May 29, 1827."

Many other similar ones might be cited from papers published in the District. The following is taken from the "Mobile (Ala.) Register" of July 21, 1837:--

"WILL BE SOLD CHEAP FOR CASH, in front of the Court-house of Mobile County, on the 22d day of July next, one mulatto-man, named Henry Hale, who says he is free. His owner or owners, if any, having failed to demand him, he is to be sold according to the statute in such case made and provided, to pay jail fees. WILLIAM MAGEE, Shff. M.C."

Here are two from the "Vicksburg (Miss.) Register." The first is the notice of the committal of a negro. The second is the advertisement for his sale:--

"SHERIFF'S SALE.--Committed to the jail of Warren County, as a runaway, on the 23d inst. a negro-man, who calls himself John J. Robinson; says that he is free; says that he kept a baker's shop in Columbus, Miss. and that he peddled through the Chickasaw nation to Pontotoc, and came to Memphis, where he sold his horse, took water, and came to this place. The owner of said boy is requested to come forward, prove property, pay charges, and take him away, or he will be dealt with as the law directs.

"Dec. 24, 1835. WM. EVERETT, Jailer."

"Notice is hereby given, that the above-described boy, who calls himself John J. Robinson, having been confined in the jail of Warren County as a runaway for six months, and having been regularly advertised during this period, I shall proceed to sell said negro-boy at public auction to the highest bidder for cash, at the door of the Court-house in Vicksburg, on Monday, 1st of August, 1836, in pursuance of the statute in such case made and provided.

"Vicksburg, July 2, 1836. E. W. MORRIS, Sheriff."

Slavery, as it exists, is not wrong, according to Bishops Ives and Freeman; and yet, in the diocese of the former, in the "Fayetteville (N.C.) Observer," June 27, 1838, this advertisement appears:--

"TAKEN AND COMMITTED TO JAIL, a negro-girl, named Nancy, who is supposed to belong to Spencer P. Wright, of the State of Georgia. She is about 30 years of age, and is a lunatic. The owner is requested to come forward, prove property, pay charges, and take her away, or she will be sold to pay her jail fees. FREDERICK HOME, Jailer."

And suppose this supposition is incorrect, and that this poor woman does not belong to Mr. Wright, but on the contrary that she is free, how then will stand the case? A poor free woman, a lunatic, one who accordingly cannot by any possibility prove her freedom, being arrested as a runaway, may be sold as a slave for life, in virtue of the laws of the Christian State of North Carolina! And no one is entitled to pronounce such act to be wrong, unless he can produce a new revelation from Heaven! If a slave has performed a great service to the State or his master, as a reward he is set free; and, if the freeman, availing himself of his privileges, goes out of his own neighborhood, the law, with the sanction of right reverend fathers in God, consigns him to the auction block!

But the runaway slave is not always to be taken easily. Strenuous liberty is often preferred to slavish ease. To meet such cases, ample provision is made, no less degrading to the slave.

If any one here at the North should advertise that he was ready to pursue, with dogs trained for the purpose, runaway apprentices, or prisoners who had escaped from jail, we should all shudder at the cold-bloodedness of the proposition. Have we not, in the Old Bay State, just solemnly enacted that not even the most hardened convicts in our State Prison shall be whipped? How, then, can we so far forget our common manhood as to pursue our brother with bloodhounds? The slave, unlike the prisoner, has committed no crime. Unlike the apprentice, he has never consented, either by himself or his parents, to be a slave. He is held in slavery against his will, and not as the punishment for any crime; and yet, if he ventures to take his freedom, to assert the highest and holiest of all his rights, he is liable to be hunted with dogs and maimed with shot! In this so-called Christian country, which is spending its millions in regenerating the heathen, whole communities exist which tolerate such a fiendish occupation as a slave-hunter! Communities do we say? Has not the nation elevated to its highest post of honor the individual who first suggested to our government the idea of importing bloodhounds from Cuba, with which to track the Seminole Indians, and the fugitive slaves whom they protected, and with whom they had intermarried? How proudly did the star-spangled banner wave its folds over the gallant men and hounds that pursued and finally conquered the panting fugitives!

In the "Madison Journal," published at Richmond, La. Nov. 26, 1847, appears the following:--

"NOTICE.--The subscriber, living on Carroway Lake, on Hoe's Bayou, in Carroll Parish, sixteen miles on the road leading from Bayou Mason to Lake Providence, is ready with a pack of dogs to hunt runaway negroes at any time. These dogs are well trained, and are known throughout the parish. Letters addressed to me at Providence will secure immediate attention.

"My terms are $5 per day for hunting the trails, whether the negro is caught or not. Where a twelve hours' trail is shown, and the negro not taken, no charge is made. For taking a negro, $25, and no charge made for hunting. JAMES W. HALL."

In the "Sumpter County Whig" (Alabama) of Nov. 6, 1845, the following is found:--

"NEGRO DOGS.--The undersigned, having bought the entire pack of negro dogs (of the Hay & Allen stock), he now proposes to catch runaway negroes. His charges will be $3 a day for hunting, and $15 for catching a runaway. He resides three and one half miles north of Livingston, near the lower Jones' Bluff road.

"Nov. 6, 1845. WILLIAM GAMBREL."

William W. Brown was hunted by Major Benjamin O'Fallon, who kept for his professional purposes five or six bloodhounds ("Narrative," p. 22). Last year, 1848, Mr. J. Ervin, a native of Fairfield District, South Carolina, a slave-hunter by profession, was murdered by some runaway slaves. Owners sometimes vary the monotony of a plantation life by a private hunt on their own account. But, unless they have considerable practice, they make a bungling piece of work of it. The true object, both of dogs and men, is the capture of the negro, not his death. Gen. Taylor did not wish to "worry" the Seminoles. We might cite many notices like the following, cut from the "Raleigh (N.C.) Register," Aug. 20, 1838:--

"On Saturday night, Mr. George Holmes, of this county, and some of his friends were in pursuit of a runaway slave (the property of Mr. Holmes), and fell in with him in attempting to make his escape. Mr. H. discharged a gun at his legs, for the purpose of disabling him; but, unfortunately, the slave stumbled, and the shot struck him near the small of the back, of which wound he died in a short time. The slave continued to run some distance after he was shot, until overtaken by one of the party. We are satisfied from all that we can learn, that Mr. H. had no intention of inflicting a mortal wound."

The hunter, in the following instance, was more skilful or lucky. The advertisement is found in the "Richmond Whig and Public Advertiser," Jan. 25, 1848:--

"$50 REWARD.--Ran away from the subscribers, on Sunday, the 8th instant, a negro-man, named George. The said slave is about 21 years of age, black, about 5 feet 6 inches high, weighs about 150 pounds, has good teeth, and a round and likely face. He was purchased at R. H. Dickinson & Bro.'s auction-room, on the 22d of March, last, from Messrs. Millner & Keen, of Pittsylvania Court-house. He was purchased by them (M. & K.) in Rickingham, N.C.; and he will in all probability make for that place, as he ran off last April, and was taken upon his way there, at Amelia Court-house. The person that took him on that occasion shot him with small shot on the legs, and the shot-marks are very perceptible on the hind part or the calves of his legs. We will give $50 for the apprehension and delivery of said boy to R. H. Dickinson & Bro. in Richmond, Va. if taken up after this date; and, if taken up previous to this date, we will pay $25 for his delivery here, and the expense of bringing him to this place from where he may be taken up. KELLY, HUNDLEY, & CO.

"Richmond, Aug. 27, 1847."

The Rev. Mr. Jones would probably instruct "George," that he was shot because he disobeyed God's commands in running away, and especially because he "robbed God of his own" in breaking the Sabbath! But how judicious was the man who took him up on that occasion! He only shot him with small shot in the legs!

In the "Macon (Ga.) Telegraph," Nov. 27, 1838, we find the following account of a runaway's den, and of the good luck of a "Mr. Adams," in running down one of them "with his excellent dogs:"--

"A runaway's den was discovered on Sunday, near the Washington Spring, in a little patch of woods, where it had been for several months so artfully concealed under ground, that it was detected only by accident, though in sight of two or three houses, and near the road and fields where there has been constant daily passing. The entrance was concealed by a pile of pine straw, representing a hog-bed, which being removed, discovered a trap-door and steps that led to a room about six feet square, comfortably ceiled with plank, containing a small fireplace, the flue of which was ingeniously conducted above ground and concealed by the straw. The inmates took the alarm, and made their escape; but Mr. Adams and his excellent dogs being put upon the trail, soon run down and secured one of them, which proved to be a negro-fellow who had been out about a year. He stated that the other occupant was a woman, who had been a runaway a still longer time. In the den was found a quantity of meal, bacon, corn, potatoes, &c. and various cooking utensils and wearing apparel."

The Lord of the sabbath seems to favor the masters; for Mr. Adams's hunt occurred on Sunday! Many other instances might be given. We adduce only this. The "St. Francisville (La.) Chronicle" of Feb. 1, 1839, gives the following account of a "negro-hunt" in that parish:--

"Two or three days since, a gentleman of this parish, in hunting runaway negroes, came upon a camp of them in the swamp on Cat Island. He succeeded in arresting two of them; but the third made fight, and, upon being shot in the shoulder, fled to a sluice, where the dogs succeeded in drowning him before assistance could arrive."

Does any one say these atrocities must be confined to the extreme South, and that law or public opinion in North Carolina would forbid them? How far otherwise is the fact! The "Revised Statutes" of North Carolina, chap. 111, sec. 22, provide as follows:--

"Whereas, many times slaves run away and lie out, hid and lurking in swamps, woods, and other obscure places, killing cattle and hogs, and committing other injuries to the inhabitants of this State; in all such cases, upon intelligence of any slave or slaves lying out as aforesaid, any two justices of the peace for the county wherein such slave or slaves is or are supposed to lurk or do mischief, shall, and they are hereby empowered and required to issue proclamation against such slave or slaves (reciting his or their names, and the name or names of the owner or owners, if known), thereby requiring him or them, and every of them, forthwith to surrender him or themselves; and also to empower and require the sheriff of the said county to take such power with him as he shall think fit and necessary for going in search and pursuit of, and effectually apprehending, such outlying slave or slaves; which proclamation shall be published at the door of the Court-house, and at such other places as said justices shall direct.[T] And if any slave or slaves against whom proclamation hath been thus issued stay out, and do not immediately return home, it shall be lawful for any person or persons whatsoever to kill and destroy such slave or slaves by such ways and means as he shall think fit, without accusation or impeachment of any crime for the same."

This is truly a Christian law! A written proclamation to men, of whom not one in ten thousand can read a letter of it!--and yet, after publication of it at the door of the Court-house, and at such other places (if any) as the justices may direct, if the slaves do not immediatelyy return, it is lawful for any person to kill and destroy them "by such ways or means as he shall think fit." And may not bloodhounds be the most expeditious and fit?

Is this law a dead letter? Only fifteen days before Bishop Freeman's sermon was delivered, and Bishop Ives enjoyed "most unfeigned pleasure" at the thought that slavery existed as it did in North Carolina, the following proclamation and advertisement appeared in the "Newbern (N.C.) Spectator:"--

"STATE OF NORTH CAROLINA, LENOIR COUNTY.--Whereas complaint hath been this day made to us, two of the justices of the peace for the said county, by William D. Cobb, of Jones county, that two negro-slaves belonging to him, named Ben (commonly known by the name of Ben Fox) and Rigdon, have absented themselves from their said master's service, and are lurking about in the counties of Lenoir and Jones, committing acts of felony; these are, in the name of the State, to command the said slaves forthwith to surrender themselves, and turn home to their said master. And we do hereby also require the sheriff of said county of Lenoir to make diligent search and pursuit after the above-mentioned slaves.... And we do hereby, by virtue of an Act of Assembly of this State concerning servants and slaves, intimate and declare, if the said slaves do not surrender themselves and return home to their master immediately after the publication of these presents, that any person may kill or destroy said slaves by such means as he or they think fit, without accusation or impeachment of any crime or offence for so doing, or without incurring any penalty or forfeiture thereby.

"Given under our hands and seals, this 12th of November, 1838.

B. COLEMAN, J.P. [Seal.] JAS. JONES, J.P. [Seal.]

"$200 REWARD.--Ran away from the subscriber, about three years ago, a certain negro-man, named Ben, commonly known by the name of Ben Fox, also one other negro, by the name of Rigdon, who ran away on the 8th of this month.

"I will give the reward of $100 for each of the above negroes, to be delivered to me, or confined in the jail of Lenoir or Jones County, or for the killing of them, so that I can see them.

"Nov. 12, 1838. W. D. COBB."

In what has preceded, we have endeavored to give a faint but true picture of slaveholding as it most generally exists. Though we have purposely left unmentioned many wrongs, we have abundantly supported our conclusion. If, as we have seen, every slave, as a man, has a natural, God-given right to be left free to seek after wisdom, to strive to become pure in heart, to cherish his affections, it is a great wrong deliberately and carefully to close against him all the avenues to knowledge, to refuse him even the rudiments imparted to the child that clings to our knees, to refuse him all moral and religious instruction, or give him such only as is calculated to make him contented with his lot, and more profitable to his oppressors. It is a great wrong--who can conceive a greater?--to deny to a whole race the sacredness of marriage, the blessings of home, the joys of brother and sister, of father and mother, and all the refining, ennobling influences of these relations. It is a great wrong, none can conceive a greater, than to trade in the bodies of men, to higgle in the market-place about the price of our brother, to traffic in our sister's flesh and bones as merchandise. Slaveholding, as it most generally exists, darkens the mind, deadens the soul, and brutalizes the affections, of its victims. It is carefully planned and deliberately executed murder of the soul. No human heart exists, unwarped by self-interest, that does not respond to the poor slave's call for help. We need no new revelation from Heaven, we need no book to tell us, that it would be wrong for any one to darken our minds, to deaden our souls, to brutalize our affections. No more do we need, a new revelation from Heaven to convince us, that all men are brethren; that the slave who toils on the Louisiana plantation is no less our neighbor than the friend whom we have known and loved from boyhood; and that we should love the slaves as ourselves, not with that barren love which consists in saving their souls by imparting to them a still more barren creed, but that love which never wearies, and which sacrifices its own for another's good.

CHAPTER X.

SLAVEHOLDING ALWAYS WRONG.

"No seeming of logic can ever convince the American people, that thousands of our slaveholding brethren are not excellent, humane, and even Christian men, fearing God, and keeping his commandments."--Rev. Dr. Joel Parker.

It remains for us to consider the special cases in which slaveholding is thought by many to be right. All slaveholders are not actors in the cruel system which we have just described. There are in the Southern States, we are ready to believe, thousands who disregard the laws, who treat their slaves as humanely as is possible, who cultivate to a considerable extent their mental and moral faculties, and who would unite with us in condemning the barbarities we have been considering.

The Rev. Dr. Richard Fuller, of Beaufort, S.C. thus describes the condition of his slaves ("Domestic Slavery considered as a Scriptural Institution," &c. p. 222; 1845):

"In a familiar correspondence like this, I may be pardoned for saying, that, during twelve years, I have devoted the salary given me, whenever at my disposal, to the spiritual instruction of the slaves, and am now doing so. With reference to my own servants, their condition is as good as I can make it. They are placed under a contract, which no instrument in writing could make more sacred. By this contract, they, on their part, perform not one half the work done by free laborers; and I, on my part, am bound to employ a missionary to teach and catechize them and their children; to provide them a home and clothes and provisions and fuel, and land to plant for themselves; to pay all medical bills; to guaranty to them all the profits of their skill and labor in their own time; to protect them as a guardian, and to administer to the wants of their children, and of those that are sick and infirm and aged. Such is their state; nor have I any idea that they would consent to be removed."

This picture may be deepened as we please. Dr. Fuller, and every slaveholder who is like him, may clothe, feed, and house his slaves as he does himself; he may watch over their mental and moral condition with as much real solicitude as he does that of a child; he may love them almost with a father's love; and yet, notwithstanding all alleviations, it is wrong for him to hold slaves. Slaveholding is always wrong.

It should be constantly borne in mind, that no man can be obliged either to become or continue a slaveholder. No man can make me a slaveholder or a landholder without or against my consent. Indeed, no gift to me of slaves or land is perfect, until I have accepted it. No man need accept an inheritance of slaves, or be a slaveholder any longer than he pleases to be. Where the law of his State permits, he may emancipate his slaves. If manumission is actually or virtually forbidden, he may take his slaves into a Free State; and, by such act alone, they become freemen. With full power, therefore, at any moment to dissolve the relation, Dr. Fuller voluntarily continues to hold slaves. All slaveholding is unnecessary, and none is involuntary on the part of the owner.

It should also be borne in mind, that a slave, under all circumstances, whether he be caressed or scourged, loved or hated, overworked or underworked, instructed or debased, is the property of his master, and, as such, is subject to all the legal incidents of property. Dr. Fuller's slaves are as much Dr. Fuller's property as his horse, his watch, the coat on his back, or the books on the shelves of his library; and, as property, their happy, elevated condition necessarily depends upon the accidents of Dr. Fuller's life, health, and wealth. When these fail, their condition will unquestionably be either very materially affected for the worse, or altogether changed.

And, first, if his wealth should fail from unforeseen calamities; so that from affluence, it may be, he should be reduced to real want, and be unable to pay the just claims of his creditors; the latter may satisfy their claims by a sale of his slaves. Nothing but payment of the debts could prevent such a catastrophe. Equally with his horses and theological library,[U] his slaves would legally constitute a fund out of which his creditors might satisfy their claims. Husband and wife, parent and child, the prattling infant and the old man of seventy winters, might legally be placed upon the auction-block, and sold to the highest bidder, singly or in lots to suit, as might seem most calculated to advance the interest of the creditors. Dr. Fuller's prayers and tears would avail nothing. His kind and humane treatment, continued through so many years, would then increase the market-value of his slaves; and that is all. Nothing that he could do would be able to save them from the auction-block. And what, under such circumstances, would become of their mental, moral, or even their physical condition? There would not be one chance in a thousand that all their new masters would be like Dr. Fuller, or that they would escape the lot of most other slaves,--a state of hopeless degradation!

Does any one say, that, though the law would favor such a sale by creditors, public opinion would not tolerate it? We will not stop to consider how far the law may be regarded as an index of public opinion. We simply ask, If Christian churches may sell slaves at auction, what may not private individuals do consistently with public opinion? We have already given the advertisement for sale by Thomas N. Gadsden, a brother, we believe, of Bishop Gadsden, of South Carolina ("Slavery as it is," p. 174), of a prime gang of negroes belonging to the Independent Church in Christ Church Parish; and we will adduce only one other similar instance. Few, if any, theological bodies at the South seem to have devoted more time, attention, and money to elevating the moral character of the slaves than the Synod of South Carolina and Georgia; and yet the Board of Directors of its Theological Seminary do not scruple to invest the funds of the institution in slaves, or to sell them by auction in order to obtain repayment of a loan. The "Savannah (Ga.) Republican" of March 3, 1845, contains an advertisement, of which the following is an extract:--

"WILL BE SOLD, on the first Tuesday in March, in front of the Court-house, in the city of Darien, Georgia, between the legal hours of sale, the following negro-slaves, i.e. Charles, Peggy, Antonett, Davy, September, Maria, Jenny, and Isaac, levied on as the property of Henry T. Hall, to satisfy a mortgage, fi. fa., issued out of the M'Intosh Superior Court in favor of the Board of Directors of the Theological Seminary of the Synod of South Carolina and Georgia, against said Henry T. Hall.--Conditions cash. C. O'NEAL, Deputy-sheriff, M.C."

Suppose Dr. Fuller should become insane, or otherwise unfit to manage his own affairs. Such cases often occur. Then the control of the slaves would pass with his other property into other hands. What would insure their continued mental and moral well-being? The law would not,--public opinion would not! Every thing would depend on the character of the legal guardian or trustee;

and even this could afford no adequate protection. The law permits an owner to do many things which it would not suffer a guardian or a trustee to do. The legal guardian of Dr. Fuller's estate would hardly be allowed to suffer his slaves to "perform not one half the work done by free laborers." The guardian's rule of conduct would be the law, and the common mode of treatment in the community. If he overstepped this line, and any pecuniary loss should be the consequence, the loss would fall on him personally. How many guardians or trustees would be willing to run any risk of a criminal prosecution or a fine or imprisonment, in order to insure the happy condition of anther's man property? Not one in ten thousand! And yet, unless his guardian was willing to do this,-- unless he was willing to brave the law, and act contrary to the general customs of society, Dr. Fuller's slaves would very soon lapse into the same degraded condition in which the slaves about them commonly live. Nothing would be more likely than to find Dr. Fuller's guardian advertising in the following manner:--

"NEGROES TO HIRE.--On Wednesday, the 26th inst. I will hire to the highest bidder the negroes belonging to Charles and Robert Innes. GEO. W. WILLIAMS, Guardian."

"NEGRO HIRINGS.--Will be offered for hire, at Capt. Long's Hotel, a number of slaves, men, women, boys, and girls, belonging to the orphans of George Ash, deceased. RICHARD W. BARTON, Guardian."

The law forbids teaching slaves to read and write. Dr. Fuller may disregard the law, and give his slaves careful instruction, supplying them with plenty of books, and allowing them time to read in. The law denies marriage to the slaves, and pays no heed to their family ties. Dr. Fuller may consecrate with the utmost care the marriage of his slaves, and sacredly protect their family relations. The law declares slaves to be, under all circumstances, saleable articles. Dr. Fuller may think that he treats them as men, and shudder at the thought of selling them. Thus may he do in his lifetime; but it is appointed unto all men to die; and what, in the event of his death, will become of his slaves?

He may possibly leave a will, bequeathing them, upon the condition that his kind and humane treatment shall be continued, that they shall be taught to read and write, that their marriages and family relations shall be sacredly respected, and that they shall never be subject to be sold; that is, on the condition that his legatees shall break the law, as he has done. The only result will be, that the law will declare all such conditions to be utterly void; and the legatees will own the slaves, entirely freed from all such conditions. The legatees will be under no other restraints than those imposed by the law, public opinion, and their own conscience. The latter restraint only may possibly avail the slaves; and their happy condition may be continued, if all the legatees are, like Dr. Fuller, law-defying, humane, kind-hearted, and above want! But how unlikely is it that such will be the case! How much more unlikely is it that such a state of things will continue! And yet, unless such a state of things exists, and continues to exist, Dr. Fuller's slaves must inevitably become as degraded as the great mass of their fellows.

If he should die intestate, then his slaves, as part of his estate, would have to be duly administered on and distributed among the heirs-at-law. The administrator, a mere trustee, could not, as we have seen, safely continue Dr. Fuller's plan of management; nor can it be supposed that any administrator would follow it. If it became necessary or expedient in order to pay debts, husbands would be separated from wives, parents from children, and brothers from sisters. The widow (if any) would be entitled to a life-estate in one-third of the slaves, which one-third would be assigned to her in severalty, even though this might involve a separation of families; for the common law of the Slave States makes the same profession as the common law of England, that it favors three things,--life, liberty, and dower! The remaining slaves, and the reversion of those assigned to the widow, would belong to the heirs, and would have to be equally divided between them, not divided by families, or even per capita, but so that each heir should have an equally valuable slave-investment, or an equal share in the property of the deceased. If the heirs should be numerous, or the slaves few, so that an equal division of them could not be thus made, they would have to be sold, and their proceeds equally divided. Such sales must be common. The following is taken from the "Georgia Journal:"--

"TO BE SOLD,--One negro-girl, about 18 months old, belonging to the estate of William Chambers, deceased. Sold for the purpose of distribution. JETHRO DEAN, } Executors." SAMUEL BEALL,}

How often are heirs needy! How very seldom are they actuated by the same spirit or governed by the same views as their ancestor! Some of them might be under age, and legally incapable of acting for themselves; and yet here, as in the other case, unless the widow and heirs-at-law should be all of full age, ready to break the law of the State, and humane, kind-hearted, and above want, like Dr. Fuller, his slaves could not escape the common degradation of their fellows. How extremely improbable is it that such would be the situation of the widow and all the heirs! How much more improbable is it that such a state of things would continue! How much more likely is it that we should find some of the heirs disliking an investment in slaves, or wishing to be disembarrassed of their care, or desirous to reduce their stock of negroes, and accordingly selling their portion of Dr. Fuller's slaves at auction! In the "Charleston (S.C.) Mercury" of Sept. 1, 1847, we find the following:--

"FOR SALE,--A young and healthy negro-woman, about 24 years of age, with her two children, a boy between 5 and 6 years, and an infant, 6 months old. Sold for no fault but to change the property. Apply at this office."

This is from the "New Orleans Commercial Bulletin" of August 27, 1847:--

"DESIRABLE VIRGINIA HOUSE-SERVANT.--By Beard, Calhoun, & Co. Saturday, 28th inst. at 12 o'clock, will be sold at auction, at Banks's Arcade, the Griffe servant, Lucy, 19 years; a trusty house-girl, of fine character, washer, ironer, and American cook, and sews remarkably well. Sold for no fault, as her owner is leaving the city. Fully guarantied against the vices and maladies prescribed by law.--Terms cash. Act of sale before J. R. Beard, notary public, at the expense of purchaser."

The "National Intelligencer" of August 1, 1848, contains the following:--

"VALUABLE SERVANT AT PRIVATE SALE.--We have for sale a valuable servant-girl, aged about 17 years. She is an excellent house-servant. Sold for no fault; the owner about removing to the country. ED. C. & G. F. DYER, Auctioneers and Commission Merchants."

The same paper of January 20, 1844, contains the following:--

"FOR SALE,--Two likely mulatto women; one middle-aged, an excellent cook, washer, and ironer, and a good seamstress; the other young, and a good seamstress and house-servant; and both capable of doing any work required in a family. They are sold on account of the owner not having sufficient employment.--Apply to Mr. Henry Trunnel, Georgetown."

In the same paper, Nov. 2, 1844, we find this:--

"A NEGRO-BOY FOR SALE OR HIRE.--A boy, 16 years old, well-grown and active, is for sale, but not to a trader. He has been employed in attending to horses, driving a carriage, working in a garden, &c. and will be sold only because the owner has too many servants. He may be had on trial.--Apply at J. B. Holmead's Auction Rooms."

The boy is not to be sold to a trader; but there can be no security that the purchaser will not thus sell him.

The "Spirit of Liberty" contains a notice, from "Scott's Intelligence Office," of the sale of three negro girls, aged 10, 19, and 16 years respectively, and a boy 14 years old. The notice states, "All the above servants are sold for no faults, and are just from the country, consigned to me for sale by their owners, who recommend them very highly; they wish to reduce their stock of negroes is the cause of their being in the market for sale."

Perhaps some one or more of Dr. Fuller's heirs may be indebted. What, in such case, will prevent a creditor from levying on an undivided share of Dr. Fuller's happy slaves? Perhaps the debtor may wish to convey his property to trustees for the benefit of his creditors. We take the following advertisement from the "National Anti-Slavery Standard," April 15, 1847:--

"TRUSTEE'S SALE.--Plantation and negroes in Washington County, Mississippi; and Yazoo city town lot and buildings. On Monday, the first of February, 1847, I will proceed to sell, by virtue of a certain deed of trust, executed 10th May, 1845, by Thomas J. Reed, to me, as trustee, and duly recorded in the proper county, and at the special instance and request of the creditors named in said deed, at public sale, to the highest bidder, for cash, on the premises, the following described lands, situated, lying, and being in the county of Washington, and State of Mississippi, and described as follows, to wit:--

"Section No. 3, &c. &c.

"Also one undivided half of the following named negroes, slaves for life, held jointly with the heirs of Baine, viz. Sophia, aged 45; Nancy, 35; Queen, 40; Jane, 19; Rachel, 11; Priscella; Jenny, 60; Maria, 30; Lydia, 30; Amanda, 22; Edna, 30; Vina, 36; Betsy, 35; Ellen, 9; Peyton, 8; Bob, 4; Louis, 15; Chub, 8; Horace, 6; Louisa, 1; Jim, jr. 4; Mary, 4-1/2; Harriet, 6; Dick, 9; George, 5; Billy, 50; John Brown, 36; Alexander, 40; Louis Johnson, 62; Hatton, 35; Jim, sen. 42; Frank, 50; John, jr. or Little John, 16; John Mitchell, 47; Louis Davis, 40; Warren, 40; Ben, 36; Oliver, 40; Louis, jr. or Charles Louis, 5; Lawson, 35; Sam, 19; Harvey, 21; Fleming, 6; Amy, 4; Bonaparte, 3; Catherine (Queen's child), 2.

"And further, all the right, title, and interest of said Reed in and to the following named slaves, to wit, Henny and her three children, Dick, Jane, and Peter; together with all the stock of horses, cattle, mules, hogs, and farming implements appertaining to said tracts of land, which is believed to be an entire estate in fee.

"The above sale will be for cash, and I will convey to the purchaser only such title as is vested in me by said deed of trust. W. S. MOTT. "No postponement on account of the weather."

Other cases might doubtless be put; but these are sufficient to enable us to test the question of right and wrong. And no labored argument is necessary. Dr. Fuller admits (what we have already proved) that slaveholding is most generally wrong, because it is accompanied by the mental and moral degradation of the slaves. But, by voluntarily retaining the ownership of his slaves, he renders just such a degradation almost inevitable even for them. Without the slightest necessity for so doing, and solely because he wishes so to do, he renders almost certain the hopeless degradation of his fellow-man. Such conduct cannot be right, even though (as doubtless in his case) pursued from right motives. No one has the right unnecessarily to impede our spiritual or mental culture, even in the slightest degree,--much less unnecessarily to expose us, almost certainly, to hopeless degradation. No more have we the right, by holding our fellows in slavery, to render almost inevitable the death of their souls.

Slaveholding, then, is always wrong, because it either deliberately murders the souls of its victims, or else renders such spiritual death almost inevitable. Nor is slaveholding ever made right by the fact that the slaves will not consent to be emancipated; for no man can rightfully consent to his own degradation. What man would consent to become even the favored slave of Dr. Fuller?

CHAPTER XI.

THE CONSTITUTION AND ITS INTERPRETATION.

The Constitution is not what it ought to be, not what we wish it to be; not what is consistent with sound morals, but simply what its words meant in 1789,--nothing more, nothing less.

The Constitution of the United States was drawn up by a Convention, of which Washington was president. The people, assembled in their State Conventions, adopted the draft, because it aptly expressed the kind of union they wished to have, because it fully and exactly expressed their meaning. In order, therefore, to ascertain the character of our political union with the Slave States, we have only to ascertain the true meaning of the words of the Constitution, or their plain, obvious, and common meaning, at the time the Constitution was adopted. Every writer who wishes to be understood uses his words in their usual signification. Every one supposes that we mean just what our words commonly mean now. When we read Chaucer, or Shakspeare, or Dr. Johnson, we understand him to mean just what his words commonly meant at the time he wrote, unless such meaning is repelled or qualified by the context, in which case we adopt this new or qualified meaning. In like manner, the people of the United States are to be understood to mean, by the words of the Constitution, just what those words commonly meant when the Constitution was adopted, unless such meaning is repelled or qualified by the context; in which case, a regard for truth obliges us to adopt this new or qualified meaning.

This simple, true, and universally practised rule is thus laid down by Judge Story (Comm. on Const. Abr. ?210):--

"Every word employed in the Constitution is to be expounded in its plain, obvious, and common sense, unless the context furnishes some ground to control, qualify, or enlarge it. Constitutions are not designed for metaphysical or logical subtleties, for niceties of expression, for critical propriety, for elaborate shades of meaning, or for the exercise of philosophical acuteness or juridical research. They are instruments of a practical nature, founded on the common business of human life, adapted to common wants, designed for common use, and fitted for common understandings. The people make them; the people adopt them; the people must be supposed to read them, with the help of common sense; and cannot be presumed to admit in them any recondite meaning, or any extraordinary gloss."--Sec. 212: "Where technical words are used, the technical meaning is to be applied to them, unless it is repelled by the context. But the same word often possesses a technical and a common sense. In such a case, the latter is to be preferred, unless some attendant circumstance points clearly to the former."

The Constitution was also framed and adopted with reference to the actual political, social, and local condition of the people. It grew out of their wants and wishes. The steps which finally led to its adoption grew out of one of the many defects in the articles of confederation. Consequently, to arrive at the true meaning of the Constitution, we must bear in mind the political, social, and local condition of the people at the time of its adoption, and, among many other similar facts, the very general existence of domestic slavery.[V]

Keeping in view these, the very simplest rules of interpretation, we will show what the Constitution is according to the common meaning of its terms; what its framers intended to make it; what, in point of fact, it has been considered to be in the practice of the government; and, finally, what it has been adjudged to mean by that body which it has itself pointed out as the final arbiter of its meaning. And, if all these unite in giving the Constitution but one character, we, as reasonable men, seeking the truth, cannot deny that such is its true character.

CHAPTER XII.

THE CONSTITUTION ACCORDING TO THE COMMON MEANING OF ITS TERMS.

The people made it, the people adopted it, the people must be supposed to read it with the help of common sense, and cannot be presumed to admit in it any hidden or extraordinary meaning.

At the time of the adoption of the Constitution, slavery existed in all the States except Massachusetts. How far, if at all, does this instrument support or countenance the institution?

Art. 1, sec. 2: "Representatives and direct taxes shall be apportioned among the several States which may be included within this union, according to their respective numbers, which shall be determined by adding to the whole number of free persons, including those bound to service for a term of years, and excluding Indians not taxed, three-fifths of all other persons."

By this section, persons are divided into those who are free and those who are slaves; for to the whole number of free persons are to be added three-fifths of all other persons, that is, persons not free, or slaves. If we adopt the plain, obvious, and common meaning of the words as their true meaning, this conclusion is incontrovertible.

It is sometimes urged, that by "free person" is meant "citizen." But the expression cannot be taken in any such technical sense. Under the expression "free persons" are included those bound to service for a term of years, and therefore from it are excluded those bound to service for life, or slaves.

This article, therefore, recognizes slavery as explicitly as if the word slave itself had been used, and gives to the free persons in a Slave State, solely because they are slaveholders, a larger representation, and consequently greater political power, than the same number of free persons in a Free State. A BOUNTY ON SLAVEHOLDING!

Art. 1, sec. 9: "The migration or importation of such persons as any of the States now existing shall think proper to admit, shall not be prohibited by the Congress prior to the year one thousand eight hundred and eight; but a tax or duty may be imposed on such importation, not exceeding ten dollars for each person."

It is clear that this section recognizes a difference between the meaning of migration and importation, since, if both words mean the same thing, no reason whatever can be assigned why a tax is not permitted in both cases. This difference, whatever it is, must afford a good reason why persons imported may be taxed, and persons migrating not. The true meaning of the section seems obvious. A person who migrates does so of his own accord: he cannot be said to be migrated by any other person. He is wholly a free agent. A person who is imported does not import himself, but is imported by some other person. He is passive. The importer is the free agent; the person imported is not a free agent. Thus the slave-laws of Virginia of 1748[W] and 1753[X] begin--"All persons who have been or shall be imported," &c. &c. "shall be accounted and be slaves." Whenever we hear an importation spoken of, we instantly infer an importer, an owner, and property imported. This distinction between the meaning of the two words is, then, real. It affords a good reason for the restriction on the right to tax. Therefore, we say, it is the true distinction. On our construction, Congress had power to lay a tax on persons imported as property or slaves, but had no right to tax free persons migrating.

By this clause, therefore, Congress was prevented, during twenty years, from prohibiting the foreign slave-trade with any State that pleased to allow it. But, by Art. 1, sec. 8, Congress had the general power "to regulate commerce with foreign nations." Consequently, the slave-trade was excepted from the operation of the general power, with a view to place the slave-trade, during twenty years, solely under the control of the Slave States. It could not be wholly stopped, so long as one State wished to continue it. It is a clear compromise in favor of slavery. True, the compromise was a temporary one; but it will be noticed, that Congress, even after 1808, was not obliged to prohibit the trade; and, in point of fact, until 1819 the laws of Congress authorized the States to sell into slavery, for their own benefit, negroes imported contrary to the laws of the United States! (Act Congr. 1807, c. 77, ?4, 6; 1818, c. 86, ?5 and 7; 10 Wheat. Rep. 321, 322.) So unmixed should be our satisfaction at the oft-repeated boast, that ours was the first nation to prohibit the African slave-trade!

Art. 4, sec. 2: "No person held to service or labor in one State, under the laws thereof, escaping into another, shall, in consequence of any law or regulation therein, be discharged from such service or labor; but shall be delivered up, on claim of the party to whom such service or labor may be due."

The time of holding not being limited, the expression here used must include not only persons held to service or labor for a term of years, but also those held to service or labor for life. Consequently, it includes those who are free persons within the meaning of Art. 1, sec. 2, and slaves or persons held to service or labor for life.

That the expression "person held to service or labor" was a correct definition of the condition of a slave, at the time the Constitution was adopted, is evident. The sixth article of the North-western ordinance reads thus: "There shall be neither slavery nor involuntary servitude in the said territory, otherwise than in the punishment of crimes, whereof the party shall have been duly convicted; provided always, that, any person escaping into the same, from whom labor or service is lawfully claimed in any one of the original States, such fugitive may be lawfully reclaimed, and conveyed to the person claiming his or her labor or service as aforesaid." In other words, the expression "a person from whom labor or service is lawfully claimed" so correctly described the condition of a slave, that Congress deemed it necessary to except such persons from the operation of an article relating only to slaves. In less than three months after the passage of this ordinance, this clause in the Constitution was drafted. It needs no argument to show, that the expression in the Constitution means the same as that in the ordinance. "A person from whom labor or service is lawfully claimed in any one of the original States" means the same as "a person held to service or labor in one State under the laws thereof." If the former correctly described the condition of a slave, the latter did also.

We can, however, see that the expression does properly describe the legal condition of a slave. A slave, though an article of property, has always and in every State been recognized as a person, by being held criminally responsible for his acts. Thus the preamble to the Act of South Carolina (May 10, 1740; 1 Grimke's Laws, 165), which provides for the trial of slaves, recites that "natural justice forbids that any person, of what condition soever, should be condemned unheard;" and the Act of Georgia of 1770 (Prince's Dig. 777) provides for the trial of "slaves and other persons." The Act of Virginia (1748, sec. 15; 5 Hen. Stat. 547) and North Carolina (1741, sec. 29; Iredell, Stat. 62-66) call runaway slaves persons in so many words. Similar laws might be cited, if deemed necessary. A slave is also held to labor and service for life by law. Labor and service are the lot of every slave. "To slave" means "to toil." It is sometimes denied, but nevertheless it is true, that the law recognizes that labor and service are legally due from the slave to his master. Thus the Act of North Carolina (1741, sec. 27), before quoted, makes it a criminal offence to tempt or persuade a slave to leave his master's "service." "Service" is recognized as being legally due from a slave in Virginia (Act 1691, 3 Hen. Stat. 86, 87). The Provincial Assembly of South Carolina (Act 1740, sec. 44) provided that,--

"If any owner of slaves, or other person who shall have the care, management, or overseeing of any slaves, shall work, or put any such slave or slaves to labor, more than fifteen hours in twenty-four hours, from the twenty-fifth day of March to the twenty-fifth day of September, or more than fourteen hours in twenty-four hours, from the twenty-fifth day of September to the twenty-fifth day of March, every such person shall forfeit any sum not exceeding twenty pounds, nor under five pounds, current money for every time he, she, or they shall offend herein, at the discretion of the justice before whom the complaint shall be made."

The Provincial Assembly of Georgia (Act 1770, May 10, sec. 41) provided that,--

"If any person shall, on the Lord's day, commonly called Sunday, employ any slave in any work or labor (works of absolute necessity and the necessary occasions of the family only excepted), every person so offending shall forfeit and pay the sum of ten shillings for every slave he, she, or they shall so cause to work or labor."

A similar law was passed in South Carolina (Act 1740, sec. 22). These and similar laws, by limiting the hours of daily work and labor, or by providing that work and labor shall not be demanded of a slave on Sunday, recognize that on other days, and within certain hours, a master may legally demand them. That which may be legally demanded is legally due. Therefore, work and labor, or service, are legally due from the slave to his master. To this labor and service the slave is "held" by the law. If he refuses to work, his master may coerce him. If he runs away, his master may pursue and retake him legally. He is "held for life," or until emancipated according to law. Consequently, the expression in the Constitution correctly describes the condition of a slave. Indeed, it more correctly describes this condition than "chattel personal" would, because it is the almost universal practice to treat a slave in many important particulars, such as dower, &c. like real property; and, in some States, slaves are declared by statute to be real estate.

By this section, therefore, it is provided that no person held as a slave in one State under the laws thereof, escaping into another, shall, in consequence of any law or regulation therein, be discharged from his slavery, but shall be delivered up on claim of his owner. The laws of one State, whether they support slavery or any other institution, have no power in another State. Consequently, if a slave escapes into a Free State, he becomes free. This is the general rule of law. In virtue of it, thousands of slaves are now free on the soil of Canada. In virtue of it, a fugitive slave from South Carolina would be free in this State, were it not for this section in the Constitution. But this section declares that he shall not thereby become free, but shall be delivered up. Again, the Constitution makes an exception from a general rule of law in favor of slavery. It gives to slaveholders, and slave-laws, a power which the general rule of law does not give. It enables a South Carolina slaveholder to drag from the soil of Massachusetts a person whom the general rule of law pronounces free, solely because South Carolina laws declare the contrary. It makes the whole Union a vast hunting-ground for slaves! There is not a single spot from the Atlantic to the Pacific, from the St. John's to the Rio del Norte, or "wheresoe'er may be the fleeting boundary of this republic," on which a fugitive slave may rest, and his owner may not, in virtue of this clause, claim and retake him as his slave!

Art. 1, sec. 8: "Congress shall have power ... to provide for calling forth the militia ... to suppress insurrections."

Art. 4, sec. 4: "The United States shall guarantee to every State in this Union a republican form of government, and shall protect each of them against invasion; and, on application of the legislature or of the executive (when the legislature cannot be convened), against domestic violence."

All insurrections and all cases of domestic violence are here provided for. To constitute an insurrection within the meaning of the Constitution, there must be a rising against those laws which are recognized as such by the Constitution; and, to make out a case of domestic violence, the violence must be exerted against that right or power which is recognized by the Constitution as lawful. But, by Art. 4, sec. 2, the Constitution admits that some persons are legally slaves; else the clause itself must be entirely inoperative. Consequently, if these persons rise in rebellion, or commit acts of violence contrary to the laws which hold them in slavery, their rising constitutes an insurrection; such acts are acts of violence within the meaning of the Constitution, and consequently must be suppressed by the national power. And what insurrections were more likely to happen and more to be dreaded than slave-insurrections, and therefore more likely to have been provided for?

Slave-owners are not the only slaveholders. All persons who voluntarily assist or pledge themselves to assist in holding persons in slavery are slaveholders. In sober truth, then, we are a nation of slaveholders! for we have bound our whole national strength to the slave-owners, to aid them, if necessary, in holding their slaves in subjection!

CHAPTER XIII.

THE CONSTITUTION AS ITS FRAMERS INTENDED TO MAKE IT.

"Yes!--it cannot be denied--the slaveholding lords of the South prescribed, as a condition of their assent to the Constitution, three special provisions to secure the perpetuity of their dominion over their slaves."--John Quincy Adams.

The question, What kind of a Constitution did its framers intend to make? is purely an historical one; and it must be obvious to all, that any thing like a complete statement of the evidence on this point cannot be given within the limits of this pamphlet.

On the 17th of September, 1787, the Philadelphia Convention adopted the plan of the present Constitution. The draft thus made was submitted to the people, assembled in State Conventions, "for their assent and ratification." President Madison has preserved a record of the debates in the Philadelphia Convention; and we have also published accounts of the debates in several of the State Conventions. We draw our evidence mainly from these sources.

APPORTIONMENT OF REPRESENTATIVES. (Const. Art. 1, sec. 2.)

On the 18th of April, 1783, the Continental Congress passed a resolve, recommending the States to amend the Articles of Confederation in such manner that the national expenses should be defrayed out of a common treasury, "which shall be supplied by the several States, in proportion to the whole number of white or other free inhabitants, of every age, sex, and condition, including those bound to servitude for a term of years, and three-fifths of all other persons not comprehended in the foregoing description, except Indians, not paying taxes, in each State." This amendment was adopted by eleven out of the thirteen States.

A single glance is sufficient to satisfy any one, that, under the expression in this resolve, "all other persons," slaves were intended; and an equally cursory glance suffices to show, that Art. 1, sec. 2, of the Constitution is derived, almost copied, from this resolve. Did not the framers of the Constitution, in adopting the same expression (Art. 1, sec. 2), mean the same thing as the Continental Congress?

In the Massachusetts Convention, Art. 1, sec. 2, of the Constitution having been read, Rufus King, one of its framers, rose to explain it:--

"This paragraph states, that the number of free persons shall be determined by adding to the whole number of free persons, including those bound to service for a term of years, and excluding Indians not taxed, three-fifths of all other persons. These persons are the slaves. By this rule is representation and taxation to be apportioned, and it was adopted because it was the language of all America....

Five negro-children of South Carolina are to pay as much tax as the three governors of New Hampshire, Massachusetts, and Connecticut."

In the New York Convention, Alexander Hamilton, another of the framers, remarked:--

"The first thing objected to is that clause which allows a representation for three-fifths of the negroes....

"The regulation complained of was one result of the spirit of accommodation which governed the Convention; and, without this indulgence, no union could possibly have been formed."

In the Pennsylvania Convention, James Wilson, another of the framers, said, referring to the resolve of the Continental Congress passed in 1783:--

"It was not carried into effect, but it was adopted by no fewer than eleven out of thirteen States; and it cannot but be matter of surprise to hear gentlemen, who agreed to this very mode of expression at that time, come forward, and state it as an objection on the present occasion. It was natural, sir, for the late Convention to adopt the mode after it had been agreed to by eleven States, and to use the expression which they found had been received as unexceptionable before."

In a speech before the legislature of Maryland, Luther Martin, also a delegate to the Philadelphia Convention, offers the following clear and unmistakable testimony:--

"With respect to that part of the second section of the first article, it was urged that no principle could justify taking slaves into computation in apportioning the number of representatives a State should have in the government;--that it involved the absurdity of increasing the power of a State in making laws for freemen, in proportion as that State violated the rights of freedom;--that it might be proper to take slaves into consideration, when taxes were to be apportioned, because it had a tendency to discourage slavery; but to take them into account in giving representation tended to encourage the slave-trade, and to make it the interest of the States to continue that infamous traffic."

In the North Carolina Convention, Wm. R. Davie, a member of the Convention who framed the Constitution, said:--

"The Eastern States had great jealousies on this subject. They insisted that their cows and horses were equally entitled to representation; that the one was property as well as the other. It became our duty, on the other hand, to acquire as much weight as possible in the legislation of the Union; and, as the Northern States were more populous in whites, this only could be done by insisting that a certain proportion of our slaves should make a part of the computed population."

In the South Carolina Convention, General Chas. C. Pinckney, another of the framers of the Constitution, said:--

"We were at a loss for some time for a rule to ascertain the proportionate wealth of the States. At last we thought that the productive labor of the inhabitants was the best rule for ascertaining their wealth. In conformity to this rule, joined to a spirit of concession, we determined that representatives should be apportioned among the several States, by adding to the whole number of free persons, three-fifths of the slaves."

PERMISSION OF THE AFRICAN SLAVE-TRADE. (Const. Art. 1, sec. 9.)

In the Massachusetts Convention, Mr. Dawes, speaking in relation to Art. 1, sec. 2, said that--

"Gentlemen would do well to connect the passage in dispute with another article in the Constitution, that permits Congress, in the year 1808, wholly to prohibit the importation of slaves, and in the meantime to impose a duty of ten dollars a head on such blacks as should be imported before that period."

Many persons spoke in the Convention on this section; and, among others, Judge Dana rejoiced that a door was opened by it for the annihilation of the slave-trade.

In the Pennsylvania Convention, Mr. Wilson said:--

"Under the present confederation, the States may admit the importation of slaves as long as they please; but by this article, after the year 1808, the Congress will have power to prohibit such importation, notwithstanding the disposition of any State to the contrary.... It is with much satisfaction I view this power in the general government, whereby they may lay an interdiction on this reproachful trade. But an immediate advantage is also obtained; for a tax or duty may be imposed on such importation, not exceeding ten dollars for each person; and this, sir, operates as a partial prohibition. It was all that could be obtained: I am sorry it was no more."

In Maryland, Luther Martin, in the speech before referred to, says, speaking of this section:--

"The design of this clause is to prevent the general government from prohibiting the importation of slaves; but the same reasons which caused them to strike out the word 'national,' and not admit the word 'stamps,' influenced them here to guard against the word 'slaves.' They anxiously sought to avoid the admission of expressions which might be odious in the ears of Americans, although they were willing to admit into their system those things which the expressions signified."

Mr. Martin thus gives the well-known history of the compromise involved in this clause:--

"This clause was the subject of a great diversity of sentiment in the Convention. As the system was reported by the committee of detail, the provision was general, that such importation should not be prohibited, without confining it to any particular period. This was rejected by eight States; Georgia, South Carolina, and, I think, North Carolina, voting for it.

"We were then told by the delegates of the two first of those States, that their States would never agree to a system which put it in the power of the general government to prevent the importation of slaves; and that they, as delegates from those States, must withhold their assent from such a system.

"A committee of one member from each State was chosen by ballot to take this part of the system under their consideration, and to endeavor to agree upon some report which should reconcile those States. To this committee also was referred the following proposition, which had been reported by the committee of detail, to wit: 'No Navigation Act shall be passed without the assent of two-thirds of the members present in each house;'--a proposition which the staple and commercial States were solicitous to retain, lest their commerce should be placed too much under the power of the Eastern States; but which these last States were as anxious to reject. This committee, of which also I had the honor to be a member, met, and took under their consideration the subjects committed to them. I found the Eastern States, notwithstanding their aversion to slavery, were very willing to indulge the Southern States, at least with a temporary liberty to prosecute the slave-trade, provided the Southern States would in their turn gratify them, by laying no restriction on Navigation Acts; and, after a very little time, the committee, by a great majority, agreed on a report, by which the general government was to be prohibited from preventing the importation of slaves for a limited time, and the restricted clause relative to Navigation Acts was to be omitted.

"This report was adopted by a majority of the Convention, but not without considerable opposition."

In the Virginia Convention, Mr. Madison said:--

"Mr. Chairman, I should conceive this clause to be impolitic, if it were one of those things which could be excluded without encountering greater evils. The Southern States would not have entered into the Union of America, without the temporary permission of that trade. And if they were excluded from the Union, the consequences might be dreadful to them and to us. We are not in a worse situation than before. That traffic is prohibited by our laws, and we may continue the prohibition. The Union in general is not in a worse situation. Under the articles of confederation, it might be continued for ever; but, by this clause, an end may be put to it after twenty years. There is, therefore, an amelioration of our circumstances. A tax may be laid in the meantime."

In the North Carolina Convention, Mr. Spaight, one of the framers of the Constitution, said--

"That there was a contest between the Northern and Southern States; that the Southern States, whose principal support depended on the labor of slaves, would not consent to the desire of the Northern States, to exclude the importation of slaves absolutely; that South Carolina and Georgia insisted on this clause, as they were now in want of hands to cultivate their lands; that in the course of twenty years they would be fully supplied; that the trade would be abolished then, and that in the meantime some tax or duty might be laid on."

In the South Carolina Convention, Hon. Rawlins Lowndes said:--

"In the first place, what cause was there for jealousy of our importing negroes? Why confine us to twenty years, or rather why limit us at all? For his part, he thought this trade could be justified on the principles of religion, humanity, and justice; for certainly to translate a set of human beings from a bad country to a better was fulfilling every part of these principles. But they don't like our slaves, because they have none themselves."

Gen. Charles C. Pinckney said:--

"By this settlement we have secured an unlimited importation of negroes for twenty years; nor is it declared that the importation shall be then stopped: it may be continued; we have a security that the general government can never emancipate them."

RESTORATION OF FUGITIVE SLAVES. (Const. Art. 4, sec. 2.)

In the Philadelphia Convention, Aug. 28, 1787, Art. 14 was taken up for consideration. This article read, "The citizens of each State shall be entitled to all privileges and immunities of citizens in the several States." Gen. Pinckney was not satisfied with it. He seemed to wish some provision should be included in favor of property in slaves.

Art. 15 was as follows:--

"Any person charged with treason, felony, or high misdemeanor, in any State, who shall flee from justice, and shall be found in any other State, shall, on demand of the executive power of the State from which he fled, be delivered up and removed to the State having jurisdiction of the offence."

This article being then taken up, the words "high misdemeanor" were struck out, and the words "other crime" inserted, in order to comprehend all proper cases; it being doubtful whether "high misdemeanor" had not a technical meaning too limited.

Mr. Butler and Mr. Pinckney moved to require "fugitive slaves and servants to be delivered up like criminals."

Mr. Wilson: This would oblige the executive of the State to do it at the public expense.

Mr. Sherman saw no more propriety in the public seizing and surrendering a slave or servant than a horse.

Mr. Butler withdrew his proposition, in order that some particular provision might be made, apart from this article.

Article 15, as amended, was then agreed to, nem. con.--Mad. Papers, pp. 1447-8.

The next day, Aug. 29, Mr. Butler, to accomplish his purpose, moved to insert, after Art. 15,--

"If any person, bound to service or labor in any of the United States, shall escape into another State, he or she shall not be discharged from such service or labor, in consequence of any regulations subsisting in the State to which they escape, but shall be delivered up to the person justly claiming their service or labor."

Which was agreed to, nem. con.

After the phraseology had been somewhat altered, on Saturday, Sept. 15, 1787, in this clause (then Const. Art. 4, sec. 2) the term "legally" was struck out, and the words "under the laws thereof" inserted after the word "State," in compliance with the wish of some one who thought the term legal equivocal, and favoring the idea that slavery was legal in a moral view.

In the Virginia Convention, Mr. Madison said:--

"Another clause secures us that property which we now possess. At present, if any slave elopes to any of those States where slaves are free, he becomes emancipated, by their laws; for the laws of the States are uncharitable (!) to one another in this respect. But in this Constitution, 'No person held to service or labor in one State, under the laws thereof, escaping into another, shall, in consequence of any law or regulation therein, be discharged from such service or labor, but shall be delivered up on claim of the party to whom such service or labor may be due.' This clause was expressly inserted to enable owners of slaves to reclaim them. This is a better security than any that now exists. No power is given to the general government to interpose with respect to the property in slaves now held by the States."

In the North Carolina Convention, Mr. Iredell begged leave to explain the reason of this clause:--

"In some of the Northern States, they have emancipated all their slaves. If any of our slaves," said he, "go there and remain there a certain time, they would, by the present laws, be entitled to their freedom, so that their masters could not get them again. This would be extremely prejudicial to the inhabitants of the Southern States; and, to prevent it, this clause is inserted in the Constitution. Though the word slave be not mentioned, this is the meaning of it. The Northern delegates, owing to their particular scruples on the subject of slavery, did not choose the word slave to be mentioned."

Gen. Pinckney, says Mr. Madison, was not satisfied with Art. 14, and "seemed to wish some provision should be included in favor of property in slaves." He thus, in the South Carolina Convention, expresses his satisfaction at this article of the Constitution:--

"We have obtained a right to recover our slaves, in whatever part of America they may take refuge, which is a right we had not before. In short, considering all circumstances, we have made the best terms for the security of this species of property it was in our power to make. We would have made better if we could; but, on the whole, I do not think them bad."(!)

SUPPRESSION OF SLAVE INSURRECTIONS. (Const. Art. 1, sec. 8; Art. 4, sec. 4.)

Luther Martin, in the speech before alluded to, used the following language:--

"It was further urged, that, by this system of government, every State is to be protected both from foreign invasion and from domestic insurrections: from this consideration, it was of the utmost importance it should have a power to restrain the importation of slaves, since, in proportion as the number of slaves are increased in any State, in the same proportion the State is weakened and exposed to foreign invasion or domestic insurrection, and by so much less will it be able to protect itself against either, and therefore will by so much the more want aid from, and be a burden to, the Union."

In the Virginia Convention, Mr. George Nicholas said:--

"Another worthy member says there is no power in the States to quell an insurrection of slaves. Have they it now? If they have, does the Constitution take it away? If it does, it must be in one of the three clauses which have been mentioned by the worthy member. The first clause gives the general government power to call them out when necessary. Does this take it away from the States? No; but it gives an additional security; for, besides the power in the State governments to use their own militia, it will be the duty of the general government to aid them with the strength of the Union, when called for. No part of this Constitution can show that this power is taken away."

Mr. Madison, respecting these clauses, says:--

"On application of the legislature or executive, as the case may be, the militia of the other States are to be called to suppress domestic insurrections. Does this bar the States from calling forth their own militia? No; but it gives them a supplementary security to suppress insurrections and domestic violence."

CHAPTER XIV.

THE CONSTITUTION ACCORDING TO THE PRACTICE OF THE GOVERNMENT.

Uniform practice under a law is one of the highest proofs of the meaning of that law.

APPORTIONMENT OF REPRESENTATIVES. (Const. Art. 1, sec. 2.)

The Constitution (Art. 1, sec. 2, par. 3) provides that the enumeration of the people of the United States (upon which the apportionment of representatives and direct taxes was to be made) "shall be made within three years after the first meeting of the Congress of the United States, and within every subsequent term of ten years, in such manner as they shall by law direct."

On the 1st of March, 1790, George Washington, who had been president of the Convention which framed the Constitution, approved "an Act providing for the enumeration of the inhabitants of the United States." The first Congress ever assembled, and the first President ever elected, under the Constitution, under the sanction of their respective oaths "to support the Constitution," by this Act expressed their deliberate judgment as to the true meaning of the people of the United States in adopting this section of the Constitution. What, in their judgment, was such meaning?

These extracts from the Act will suffice (Act 1790, chap. 29):--

Sec. 1: "Be it enacted, &c. That the marshals of the several districts of the United States shall be, and they are hereby, authorized and required to cause the number of the inhabitants within their respective districts to be taken, omitting, in such enumeration, Indians not taxed, and distinguishing free persons, including those bound to service for a term of years, from all others; distinguishing also the sexes and colors of free persons, and the free males of sixteen years and upwards from those under that age: for effecting which purpose, the marshals shall have power to appoint as many assistants within their respective districts as to them shall appear necessary, assigning to each assistant a certain division of his district," &c.

These assistants were obliged to transmit to the marshals, returns in manner following:--

"The number of persons within my division, consisting of ----, appears in a schedule hereunto annexed, subscribed by me, this ----day of ---- 179 .

A. B. Assistant to the Marshal of ----"

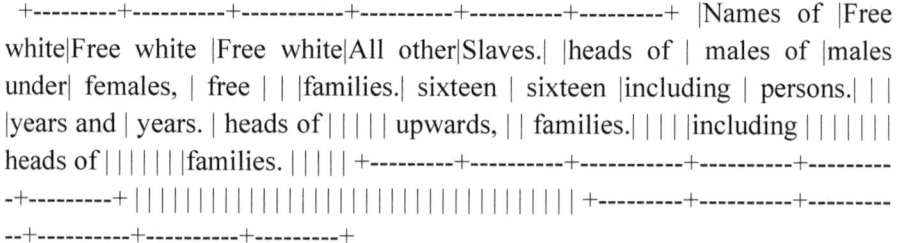

+---------+----------+-----------+----------+----------+---------+ |Names of |Free white|Free white |Free white|All other|Slaves.| |heads of | males of |males under| females, | free | | |families.| sixteen | sixteen |including | persons.| | | |years and | years. | heads of| | | | | upwards, | | families.| | | | |including | | | | | heads of| | | | | | |families. | | | | | +---------+----------+-----------+----------+---------+ | | | | | | | | | | | | | | | | | | | | | | | | | | | | | | | | | | | | | | | | | +---------+----------+-----------+----------+---------+

That is, the enumeration directed to be made, and upon the basis of which the constitutional apportionment of representatives and direct taxes was to be made, distinguished only between free persons and slaves. Congress and the President, under the sanction of their oaths, united in the expression of their deliberate judgment, that the people of the United States, by the expression (Art. 1, sec. 2) "three-fifths of all other persons," intended "three-fifths of the slaves," because, in passing this Act, they declare that all other persons not free within the meaning of this section are slaves.

The second Congress, at its first session, passed "An Act for apportioning representatives among the several States, according to the first enumeration" (Stat. 1792, c. 23). The language of the statute is as follows:--

Sec. 1: "Be it enacted, &c. That from and after the third day of March, one thousand seven hundred and ninety-three, the House of Representatives shall be composed of members elected agreeably to a ratio of one member for every thirty-three thousand persons in each State, computed according to the rule prescribed by the Constitution, that is to say, within the State of New Hampshire, four," &c. &c.

That is, the second Congress, upon an enumeration distinguishing only freemen from slaves, undertake to apportion representatives among the States according to the rule laid down in the Constitution, viz. by adding to the whole number of free persons "three-fifths of the slaves."

This interpretation, by the first and second Congress, has never been varied from. In every census which has since been taken, the only distinction sanctioned has been between freemen and slaves; and, on every occasion of apportioning representatives, according the representative or federal number, such number has been invariably determined by adding to the whole number of free persons, three-fifths of the slaves. If this, the pro-slavery, interpretation of this section of the Constitution is not right, then, since March 3, 1793, there has not been a single House of Representatives constitutionally elected, or a single statute or resolve constitutionally passed! Who is ready to make this admission?

PERMISSION OF THE AFRICAN SLAVE-TRADE. (Const. Art. 1, sec. 9.)

On the 13th of May 1789, in Congress,--

"Mr. Parker (of Va.) moved to insert a clause in the bill, imposing a duty on the importation of slaves of ten dollars each person. He was sorry that the Constitution prevented Congress from prohibiting the importation altogether; he thought it a defect in that instrument that it allowed of such actions; it was contrary to the revolution principles, and ought not to be permitted; but, as he could not do all the good he desired, he was willing to do what lay in his power.

* * * * *

"Mr. Sherman (of Ct.) approved of the object of the motion; but he did not think this bill was proper to embrace the subject. He could not reconcile himself to the insertion of human beings, as an article of duty, among goods, wares, and merchandise. He hoped it would be withdrawn for the present, and taken up hereafter as an independent subject.

* * * * *

"Mr. Schureman (of N. J.) hoped the gentleman would withdraw his motion, because the present was not the time or place for introducing the business; he thought it had better be brought forward in the House, as a distinct proposition.

* * * * *

"Mr. Madison (of Va.): I cannot concur with gentlemen who think the present an improper time or place to enter into a discussion of the proposed motion. If it is taken up in a separate view, we shall do the same thing, at a greater expense of time....

"I conceive the Constitution, in this particular, was formed in order that the government, whilst it was restrained from laying a total prohibition, might be able to give some testimony of the sense of America with respect to the African trade. We have liberty to impose a tax or duty upon the importation of such persons as any of the States now existing shall think proper to admit; and this liberty was granted, I presume, upon two considerations: the first was, that, until the time arrived when they might abolish the importation of slaves, they might have an opportunity of evidencing their sentiments on the policy and humanity of such a trade; the other was, that they might be taxed in due proportion with other articles imported; for, if the possessor will consider them as property, of course they are of value, and ought to be paid for."

After a very considerable discussion, in which this section of the Constitution was referred to by various members, and the constitutionality of Mr. Parker's motion admitted, with the advice of Mr. Madison his colleague, Mr. Parker consented to withdraw his motion.

In 1794, "An Act to prohibit the carrying on the slave-trade from the United States to any foreign place or country" was passed (Stat. 1794, c. 11). In 1800, an Act in addition to the last was passed (Stat. 1800, c. 51). That both these laws were framed with reference to this section of the Constitution is apparent, because the latter Act expressly refers to it. Sec. 6 reads thus, "That nothing in this Act contained shall be construed to authorize the bringing into either of the United States any person or persons, the importation of whom is, by the existing laws of such State, prohibited." In 1803 (Stat. 1803, c. 63) was passed "An Act to prevent the importation of certain persons into certain States, where, by the laws thereof, their admission is prohibited."

Sec. 1: "Be it enacted, &c. That, from and after the first day of April next, no master or captain of any ship or vessel, or any other person, shall import or bring, or cause to be imported or brought, any negro, mulatto, or other person of color, not being a native, a citizen, or registered seaman of the United States, or seamen, natives of countries beyond the Cape of Good Hope, into any port or place of the United States, which port or place shall be situated in any State which by law has prohibited, or shall prohibit, the admission or importation of such negro, mulatto, or other person of color," &c. &c.

This Act also is most manifestly framed upon this section of the Constitution. It renders illegal the importation of any negro, mulatto, or person of color, into States prohibiting such importation, unless such negro, &c. is a native, citizen, or registered seaman of the United States, or native of countries beyond the Cape of Good Hope; that is, it renders illegal the importation of African negroes into any State whose laws prohibit such importation. And, as no African negro has yet been imported as a free laborer, this Act was directed against the African slave-trade.

And, not to multiply proof, the importation of persons is not to be prohibited by Congress prior to 1808. On the 2d day of March, 1807, President Jefferson approved (Stat. 1807, c. 77) "An Act to prohibit the importation of slaves into any port or place within the jurisdiction of the United States, from and after the first day of January, in the year of our Lord one thousand eight hundred and eight." That is, at the very earliest day allowed by Const. Art. 1, sec. 9, for the passage by Congress of an Act prohibiting the importation of persons, a law is passed totally prohibiting the importation of slaves.

RESTORATION OF FUGITIVE SLAVES. (Const. Art. 4, sec. 2.)

On the 12th day of February, 1793 (Stat. 1793, chap. 7), there was approved "An Act respecting fugitives from justice, and persons escaping from the service of their masters." This is the law which, for over half a century, has prescribed the modes in which a runaway slave may be retaken. It is what is now called "the infamous law of '93." Thousands of runaway slaves have owed their return to their happy condition to the beneficent operation of this law, obviously framed, as it is, with an eye to this constitutional provision.

Sec. 3 provides that,--

"When a person held to labor in any of the United States, or in either of the territories on the north-west or south of the river Ohio, under the laws thereof, shall escape into any other of the said States or territory, the person to whom such labor or service may be due, his agent or attorney, is hereby empowered to seize or arrest such fugitive from labor, and to take him or her before any judge of the circuit or district courts of the United States, residing or being within the State, or before any magistrate of a county, city, or town corporate, wherein such seizure or arrest shall be made; and, upon proof to the satisfaction of such judge or magistrate, either by oral testimony or affidavit, taken before and certified by a magistrate of any such State or territory, that the person so seized or arrested doth, under the laws of the State or territory from which he or she fled, owe service or labor to the person claiming him or her, it shall be the duty of such judge or magistrate to give a certificate thereof to such claimant, his agent or attorney, which shall be sufficient warrant for removing the said fugitive from labor to the State or territory from which he or she fled."

SUPPRESSION OF SLAVE INSURRECTIONS. (Const. Art. 1, sec. 8; Art. 4, sec. 4.)

"An Act to provide for calling forth the militia to execute the laws of the Union, suppress insurrections, and repel invasions," was approved May 2, 1792 (Act Const. 1792, chap. 28). Section first provides that, "In case of an insurrection in any State against the government thereof, it shall be lawful for the President of the United States, on application of the legislature of such State, or of the executive (when the legislature cannot be convened), to call forth such number of the militia of any other State or States as may be applied for, or as he may judge sufficient to suppress such insurrection." Precisely the same language is made use of in Stat. 1795, c. 101. By Act approved March 3, 1807 (Stat. 1807, c. 94), the President is authorized "in all cases of insurrection," "when it is lawful for him to call forth the militia for the purpose of suppressing the same," "to employ for the same purpose such part of the land or naval force of the United States as shall be judged necessary."

That these laws have been held to include an insurrection of slaves is indisputable. On receipt of the intelligence of Nat. Turner's insurrection in Southampton, Va., Col. House, then commanding at Fortress Monroe, set out with three companies of United States troops, for the purpose of suppressing the revolt. He was reinforced by a detachment from the United States ships Warren and Natchez, amounting in all to about three hundred men. With our troops and our officers we have actually aided the slaveholder in holding his fellow-man in slavery! We have actually done what our fathers engaged in the Constitution that we should do, namely, aid with the national strength in keeping the slaves in subjection!

CHAPTER XV.

THE CONSTITUTION ACCORDING TO THE EXPOSITION OF ITS FINAL INTERPRETER.

"The judicial department of the United States is, in the last resort, the final expositor of the Constitution as to all questions of a judicial nature. Were there no power to interpret, pronounce, and execute the law, the government would either perish through its own imbecility, as was the case with the articles of confederation, or other powers must be assumed by the legislative body, to the destruction of liberty."--Chancellor Kent.

The people of the United States, in adopting the Constitution, made one standard, one fundamental law, and only one. They gave to the government of the United States certain powers. They restricted it as to others. They placed certain prohibitions on the States. The Constitution was to be the one fundamental law of the land, to which all, as well States as people, should submit. Art. 6, sec. 2, provides that the "Constitution and the laws of the United States which shall be made in pursuance thereof, and all treaties made, or which shall be made, under the authority of the United States, shall be the supreme law of the land; and the judges in every State shall be bound thereby, any thing in the Constitution or laws of any State to the contrary notwithstanding."

Who now is to tell us what this one standard is, to which all must submit, and which is thus to override all State Constitutions and all State laws? Is it the province of each individual to do it? Then we may have at this moment seventeen million different interpretations, and hence as many different Constitutions, each of which, however, is the supreme law of the land! Are the executive or judicial departments of the States the proper expounders? Then, at this moment, we may have only thirty different interpretations, twenty-nine of which must be wrong, because the supreme law can be but one.

In order, therefore, that the end of the Constitution may be accomplished, that it may really be the supreme law of the land, it must have provided a way in which its only true meaning may be ascertained and definitively settled. Unless it has provided a final interpreter of its meaning, it is the merest folly to style it the supreme law of the land, or to call on us to obey its requirement. Is the Constitution thus deficient? Does it demand uniformity, and at the same time deny the use of those means which are absolutely necessary to produce such uniformity? Does it present a variable, ever-changing standard of duty, and yet demand complete uniformity in practice?

There are three departments in the Government, namely, the Executive, the Legislative, and the Judicial. The first two of these are each, to some extent, supreme in its own sphere; and its acts are incapable of revision elsewhere. "Thus, in measures exclusively of a political, legislative, or executive character, it is plain, that, as the supreme authority as to these questions belongs to the legislative and executive departments, they cannot be re-examined elsewhere. Thus, Congress having the power to declare war, to levy taxes, to appropriate money, to regulate intercourse and commerce with foreign nations, their mode of executing these powers can never become the subject of re-examination in any other tribunal. So, the power to make treaties being confided to the President and Senate, when a treaty is properly ratified, it becomes the law of the land, and no other tribunal can gainsay its stipulations. Yet cases may readily be imagined, in which a tax may be laid, or a treaty made, upon motions and grounds wholly beside the intention of the Constitution. The remedy, however, in such cases is solely by an appeal to the people at the elections, or by the salutary power of amendment provided by the Constitution itself.

"But, where the question is of a different nature, and capable of judicial inquiry and decision, there it admits of a very different consideration. The decision then made, whether in favor or against the constitutionality of the Act, by the State or by national authority, by the legislature or by the executive, being capable in its own nature of being brought to the test of the Constitution, is subject to judicial revision. It is in such cases, as we conceive, that there is a final and common arbiter provided by the Constitution itself, to whose decisions all others are subordinate; and that arbiter is the supreme judicial authority of the courts of the Union" (Story, Comm. Const. sec. 374, 375); for the Constitution declares, Art. 3, sec. 2, that "the judicial power shall extend to all cases in law and equity arising under this Constitution, the laws of the United States, and treaties made, or which shall be made, under their authority," &c. And Art. 3, sec. 1: "The judicial power of the United States shall be vested in one supreme court, and in such inferior courts as the Congress may from time to time ordain and establish."

These constitutional provisions are clear. The Constitution and laws and treaties of the United States are declared to be the supreme law of the land. To expound what the law is, is a judicial act. The judicial power extends to all cases arising under the Constitution, laws, and treaties of the United States. It therefore extends to the exposition of the Constitution, laws, and treaties, when the case before the court properly calls for such exposition. This judicial power, and consequently this power of exposition, it is declared, shall be vested in one supreme court, &c. Most obviously, the exposition given by this one supreme court cannot be overruled by any other constitutional power; else the court is not supreme, else the Constitution is nullified. The decision of the supreme court is the decision of the only constitutionally authorized expounder of the meaning of the Constitution; and such exposition, to be supreme, must be final.

What, then, has this final interpreter declared the meaning of these clauses of the Constitution to be?

APPORTIONMENT OF REPRESENTATIVES. (Const. Art. 1, sec. 2.)

On the 5th of June, 1794 (Stat. 1794, c. 45), was approved an Act of Congress, "laying duties upon carriages for the conveyance of persons." The duty was uniform throughout the States. One Hylton, in Virginia, refused to pay the duty; alleging that the Act was unconstitutional, because the tax was a direct tax within the meaning of the Constitution, and therefore should have been apportioned among the States according to their federal numbers. He was sued by the United States, and finally the case came before the supreme court of the United States for decision. The following extracts are taken from the opinion of Justice Paterson (Hylton versus the United States, 3 Dallas's Reports, p. 177; 1796):--

"I never entertained a doubt that the principal, I will not say the only, objects that the framers of the Constitution contemplated, as falling within the rule of apportionment, were a capitation-tax and a tax on land. Local considerations, and the particular circumstances and relative situation of the States, naturally lead to this view of the subject. The provision was made in favor of the Southern States. They possessed a large number of slaves; they had extensive tracts of territory, thinly settled, and not very productive. A majority of the States had but few slaves; and several of them, a limited territory, well-settled, and in a high state of cultivation. The Southern States, if no provision had been introduced in the Constitution, would have been wholly at the mercy of the other States. Congress, in such case, might tax slaves at discretion or arbitrarily, and land in every part of the Union. After the same rate or measure, so much a head in the first instance, and so much an acre in the second. To guard them against imposition in these particulars was the reason of introducing the clause in the Constitution which directs that representatives and direct taxes shall be apportioned among the States, according to their respective numbers."

Page 178: "The rule of apportionment is of this nature: it is radically wrong; it cannot be supported by any solid reasoning. Why should slaves, who are a species of property, be represented more than any other property? The rule, therefore, ought not to be extended by construction."

PERMISSION OF THE AFRICAN SLAVE-TRADE. (Const. Art. 1, sec. 9.)

In the great case of Gibbons vs. Ogden, 9 Wheaton's Reports, pp. 206 and 207 (1824), Chief Justice Marshall, delivering the opinion of the supreme court, makes use of the following language:--

"The Act passed in 1803 (Act Const. 1803, c. 63), prohibiting the importation of slaves into any State which shall itself prohibit their importation, implies, it is said, an admission that the States possess the power to exclude or admit them; from which it is inferred, that they possess the same power with respect to other articles.

"If this inference were correct; if this power were exercised, not under any particular clause in the Constitution, but in virtue of a general right over the subject of commerce to exist as long as the Constitution itself, it might now be exercised. Any State might now import African slaves into its own territory. But it is obvious that the power of the States over this subject, previous to the year 1808, constitutes an exception to the power of Congress to regulate commerce; and the exception is expressed in such words as to manifest clearly the intention to continue the pre-existing right of the States to admit or exclude for a limited period. The words are, 'The migration or importation of such persons as any of the States now existing shall think proper to admit, shall not be prohibited by the Congress prior to 1808.' The whole object of the exception is to preserve the power to those States which might be disposed to exercise it, and its language seems to the court to convey this idea unequivocally."

See also pp. 216, 217.

RESTORATION OF FUGITIVE SLAVES. (Const. Art. 4, sec. 2.)

The following extracts are taken from the opinion of the supreme court in the well-known case, Prigg vs. the Commonwealth of Pennsylvania (16 Pet. Rep. 609, &c.). Judge Story delivered the opinion:--

"Historically, it is well known, that the object of this clause was to secure to the citizens of the slaveholding States the complete right and title of ownership in their slaves, as property, in every State in the Union into which they might escape from the State where they were held in servitude. The full recognition of this right and title was indispensable to the security of this species of property in all the slaveholding States; and, indeed, was so vital to the preservation of their domestic interests and institutions, that it cannot be doubted that it constituted a fundamental article, without the adoption of which the Union could not have been formed. Its true design was to guard against the doctrines and principles prevalent in the non-slaveholding States, by preventing them from intermeddling with, or obstructing, or abolishing, the rights of the owners of slaves."

Page 612: "If the Constitution had not contained this clause, every non-slaveholding State in the Union would have been at liberty to have declared free all runaway slaves coming within its limits, and to have given them entire immunity and protection against the claims of their masters;--a course which would have created the most bitter animosities, and engendered perpetual strife, between the different States. The clause was, therefore, of the last importance to the safety and security of the Southern States, and could not have been surrendered by them without endangering their whole property in slaves. The clause was accordingly adopted into the Constitution by the unanimous consent of the framers of it;--a proof at once of its intrinsic and practical necessity."

Page 613: "Upon this ground, we have not the slightest hesitation in holding, that, under and in virtue of the Constitution, the owner of a slave is clothed with entire authority, in every State in the Union, to seize and recapture his slave, whenever he can do it without any breach of the peace or any illegal violence. In this sense, and to this extent, this clause of the Constitution may properly be said to execute itself, and to require no aid from legislation, state or national."

Page 625: "Upon these grounds, we are of opinion, that the Act of Pennsylvania upon which this indictment is founded is unconstitutional and void. It purports to punish, as a public offence against that State, the very act of seizing and removing a slave by his master, which the Constitution of the United States was designed to justify and uphold."

SUPPRESSION OF SLAVE INSURRECTIONS. (Const. Art. 1, sec. 8; Art. 4, sec. 4.)

We are not aware of any decision of the supreme court upon the meaning of these clauses; but it seems difficult to conceive, that they would hold that the word "insurrections" did not include all insurrections.

* * * * *

Such is the Constitution according to the plain, obvious, and common meaning of its terms; such it was intended to be made by its framers; such has been the interpretation constantly followed in the practice of the government, from the time of its adoption until now; and such it is according to the decision of the final interpreter of its meaning. As reasonable men, seeking the truth, we cannot say that there is the slightest doubt whatever on the subject. THE CONSTITUTION VERY MATERIALLY SUPPORTS SLAVERY!

CHAPTER XVI.

NO UNION WITH SLAVEHOLDERS.

"We will extend to the slaveholder all the courtesy he will allow. If he is hungry, we will feed him; if he is in want, both hands shall be stretched out for his aid. We will give him full credit for all the good that he does, and our deep sympathy in all the temptations under whose strength he falls. But to help him in his sin, to remain partners with him in the slave-trade, is more than he has a right to ask."--Wendell Phillips.

No wrong action can be rightfully done. No wrong can be rightfully supported. We can neither rightfully hold slaves nor support others in slaveholding, because, as we have seen, slaveholding is under all circumstances wrong. Some of the provisions of the Constitution, as we have seen, were expressly designed for the purpose of supporting slavery, and for over half a century have very materially supported it. Consequently, these provisions cannot be rightfully obeyed or supported. It is wrong to offer a bounty on slaveholding,--to give the oppressor power and influence, in proportion as he tramples on the rights of his fellow-man; it is wrong to return, or aid in returning, a fugitive slave; it is wrong to aid in keeping the slave in his fetters. These things are wrong, and not all the Constitutions and laws of the universe can make them right. We cannot, therefore, rightfully obey the pro-slavery clauses of the Constitution.

If we cannot rightfully obey them ourselves, we cannot rightfully, voluntarily support others in obeying them. If it is wrong for me to return a fugitive slave, it is wrong for me voluntarily to aid or support another man in doing the act. If it is wrong for me to commit murder, it is no less wrong for me to hand the pistol to the assassin. Whatever it is wrong for us to do ourselves, it is wrong for us voluntarily to aid or support others in doing. Consequently, it is wrong for us voluntarily to aid or support others in obeying the pro-slavery requirements of the Constitution.

If we cannot rightfully obey them, it is wrong for us to promise such obedience. If it is wrong for us voluntarily to support others in their obedience, it is wrong for us to promise any such support. If it is wrong for us to return a fugitive slave, it is wrong for us to promise to return one. If it is wrong for us voluntarily to aid the slave-hunter, it is wrong for us to promise such aid. Whatever it is wrong for us to do or aid others in doing, it is wrong for us to promise to do or aid others in doing. Consequently, it is wrong for us to promise to support these constitutional provisions. We cannot, therefore, accept any office, either state or national, which renders it necessary for us to support these clauses, or to promise to support them. We cannot, therefore, rightfully hold any executive or judicial office, either state or national, or become a member of any State legislature or of Congress; for all these officers are obliged solemnly to swear or affirm that they will "support the Constitution;" and to support the Constitution is to support all of its clauses, as well those which favor slavery as those which do not. If we take this oath, meaning to keep it, we do wrong. If we take it, meaning not to keep it, we add to our wrong, perjury; for we mentally break our oath at the very instant it passes our lips.

Some good men seek to avoid the difficulty by saying, "When I swear to support the Constitution, I mean I will support the good clauses in it, and disobey the bad, and submit to the penalty for such disobedience." But such a course is not a compliance with the terms of the oath. You have sworn "to support the Constitution;" that is, the whole Constitution,--all its clauses,--the bad as sacredly as the good. Your oath is not in the alternative, "I will support the clause requiring the return of fugitive slaves, or pay five hundred dollars for every slave I aid in escaping;" but simply, without any qualification, "I will support the side of the oppressor." If you aid the fugitive slave to escape from his master, you do not support the latter in retaking his property, merely by paying the legal penalty for not giving such support. You would not support a bad law, and yet you say your oath to support it is not broken, because you submit to the penalty for not supporting it. The thief does not support the law of private property, merely by submitting to the legal punishment of his crime. To support is to be active: to submit is to be passive. You swear to be active, and you do not comply with your oath by being merely passive. You have sworn actively to support the recapture of slaves. You break your oath, if you refuse to do this, or do any thing less or different from this.

Others think to find a good excuse for taking the oath, by adopting another alternative, equally unauthorized. "We will support the Constitution," say they, "until we are called on to act under any of its bad clauses; and then we will resign our office, and refuse obedience." Doubtless, honor requires you to resign, if you cannot comply with the terms of your oath; but what right have you to adopt or imagine an alternative in your oath where the law has made none,--where the officer administering it will admit of none? Who does not see the wide difference between an honest oath to support the return of fugitive slaves, and an oath to support such return, but with a firm resolve on your part to refuse such support when called on for it, and to resign? What right have you to take an oath which you have previously resolved not to keep, when called on to comply with? You admit that a bad clause cannot be rightfully supported, else why do you not support it? You admit that the oath obliges you to support the bad clauses of the Constitution as well as the good; else why do you resign, if refusal to support the bad clauses is consistent with your oath? You openly avow, therefore, that, at the very moment you swear to support a clause, you determine never to support it. You swear, and determine not to keep your oath! Such a course seems to us inconsistent with the plainest rules of honesty. We have no right to promise to do wrong, even though we have resolved to do right when the time for action shall arrive.

Others say, "We swear to support the Constitution as we understand it, and we consider it an anti-slavery instrument." In other words, you swear to support an interpretation which is contrary to the plain, obvious, and common meaning of the instrument; contrary to the interpretation put upon it by its framers; contrary to that followed by all the executive and legislative departments of the government, from its first establishment until now; and contrary to that which has been adjudged to be its true interpretation by the final arbiter of its meaning. Of course, you intend to support the true meaning of the Constitution. Do you really believe that the people of the United States did not mean by their words what those words then commonly meant? Do you really doubt the historical fact of the humiliating compromise between the delegates from the Southern and Eastern States in the Philadelphia Convention, by which the latter undertook to barter the moral sense of their constituents for what was supposed to be their interest? Do you really believe that the people have suffered their servants to go on in ignorance of the true meaning for sixty years? In fact, do you venture to affirm, or do you in perfect sincerity and truthfulness believe, that your interpretation has ever at any time been considered right by the people of the United States, or by any considerable number of them? You deceive yourself with words! What is the Constitution? Not the meaning which you or I, or any third person, may please to put upon it; but that meaning, and that meaning only, which consists with its being, what it declares itself to be, the supreme law of the land. Until, therefore, you can show that the Constitution may properly receive as many different interpretations as there are oaths to support it, and still be in fact the supreme law, the one, single, definite rule for all, States as well as people, you have no right to say, "I will support the pro-slavery clauses as I understand them." To support them in any other sense than that which is affixed to them, as the supreme law of the land, is merely to evade the true meaning of your oath.

Others say, "We took the oath before we had any of our present scruples. We would not take the oath now; but, nevertheless, we shall continue in office, and disregard our oath." This excuse seems to us very objectionable. How can you reap the honorary or pecuniary advantages of your office, and honestly refuse compliance with your part of the bargain? When you took office, you were really told, that, if you would swear to support the return of fugitive slaves, &c. you should enjoy these honors and these profits. The conscientious man, who, in striving to better himself, not his condition, discovers afterwards that he cannot rightfully aid, or promise to aid, the slaveholder in retaking his slaves, will not think of claiming the reward which was offered to him solely because he swore to give such aid. He will make haste to resign honors and rewards which he feels can be retained only at the price of his own degradation.

If we cannot rightfully hold any office, state or national, which requires of us a promise to support the Constitution, it is wrong to place, or voluntarily aid in placing, any other person in such office; for, by so doing, we ask him to do wrong. If we vote for Horace Mann, by this act alone we say to him, as distinctly as if the words passed our lips,--"We wish to elect you as representative to Congress. If chosen, we expect and ask you to qualify yourself to act as representative, by swearing to give slavery all constitutional support." Merely by voting for him, we ask him to do wrong, hoping that good may come, almost knowing that good will come! So little faith have we in the final triumph of right and justice, by pursuing only right and just ways! Of so little consequence do we consider it, that the earnest advocate of freedom should commence his holy work by promising very materially to strengthen slavery! But a short time has elapsed since we read one of his most eloquent rebukes of slavery. Our heart beat quickly as we read his earnest words. But if, in the midst of his address, some slaveholder had turned and asked him, "How happens it, sir, that you, who are so very earnest and disinterested in behalf of the rights of the slave, have been willing to swear to support this terrible wrong, to any extent or for any time?" And what answer could be returned? The eloquent tongue would be palsied! Surely that man who has solemnly called God to witness that he will support the oppressor, cannot fail, at some time or another, to feel himself to be unworthy to plead the cause of freedom.

Finally, some say, "This reasoning leads to non-resistance. You disregard the fact that all human governments must contain a greater or less amount of evil; and consequently, if you are ever to support any government in all its requirements, you must support evil." Very true is it that human governments and laws fall short of our relative standard of right, and always of absolute right. What is our duty? Clearly, as moral beings, to support the right, and refuse to support the wrong; as peaceful citizens, to support the right, and submit to the penalty of disobeying the wrong. Nothing more than this is required of us. Nothing less than this is our duty. We are not put into the world, blindly to support all existing governmental wrongs, until they can be constitutionally abolished. We are to be true to ourselves as moral beings. If we can be true to our own souls and support the government, we may give such support,--not otherwise! Right and wrong are not creatures of agreement and law. Neither the Philadelphia Convention that framed the Constitution, nor the State Conventions that adopted it, had power to make wrong in the slightest degree right, or alter at all the moral character of slaveholding. Right is right, the Revised Statutes to the contrary notwithstanding. Wrong is wrong, the Constitution to the contrary notwithstanding. We say, therefore, we will obey the good requirements of the Constitution, and peacefully submit to the penalty of disobeying the bad. This is all that government has a right to ask of us. Institutions were made for man, not man for them. Constitutions are the work of man, and man is to be reverenced before his works. We see no inconsistency or impropriety in supporting the system of free-trade between the States, and refusing to support the domestic slave-trade; in supporting the patent laws, and refusing to aid in returning a runaway slave. We are good-government men, not no-government men. All governments are partly good. All we are willing to support in part: we will actively support the Constitution and laws, so far as conscience permits; we will peacefully submit to legal exaction for disobeying the rest.

Our purpose is accomplished. We have shown that we are politically united with the South in the support of slavery. We have shown that we should constantly bear upon our lips, and in our lives, the motto, "No union with slaveholders, whereby we are obliged to countenance or support slavery." We desire to see a union among the States, but not a slaveholding union! A union of freemen, and Free States for the sake of freedom, no one would more readily support than we. But a union like ours, of freemen and slaveholders, of Free States and Slave States, for the sake in part of securing property in slaves, is demoralizing (how demoralizing has it been!) to both parties, and should receive, as it doubtless at no distant day will receive, the condemnation of the wise and good. In the meantime, it ought not, and it will not, receive either our respect or our voluntary support.

FOOTNOTES:

[A] Mr. Clapp is said to have changed his opinions since 1838. We hope he has. But he has not favored the world with any statement of what his change consists in. The statement which recently appeared in the "Picayune," even if reliable, shows that Mr. Clapp had changed his opinion somewhat, but not essentially, as it seems to us.

[B] We quote from Mr. Jones's work just referred to. His work contains a summary of all that has been done for the religious instruction of the negroes from their first introduction here; an account of their actual moral condition, and what he thinks should be done for their elevation. His testimony is unimpeachable, and is of the very highest authority. Our faith in his sincerity is sometimes tried, when we read language like this applied to the adult slave, p. 117: "He marries and settles in life; his children grow up around him, and tread in his footsteps, as he did in the footsteps of his father before him."

For a loan of this book we are indebted to the kindness of our friend, William Lloyd Garrison.

[C] Sandy Jenkins tried to impress Douglass with the belief, that if he would always carry a root which he gave him, on his right side, it would render it impossible for any white man to whip him ("Narrative," p. 70). And before Wm. W. Brown made his last successful effort to escape, he paid the old slave fortune-teller, Frank, twenty-five cents for his advice.

[D] "If they make you partakers of their temporal things (of their strength and spirits, and even of their offspring), you ought to make them partakers of your spiritual things."--Bishop of London in 1727 (Jones, p. 20).

[E] How carefully does Mr. Jones teach the slaves "to search the Scriptures"! ("Catechism," p. 103.)

"Q. Is not our duty, on the sabbath, to go to the house of God, to the meeting for prayer, to the sabbath-school, and wherever we may worship God and learn his will?--A. Yes.

"Q. What was done with the man that gathered sticks on the sabbath-day, not caring for God's commandment?--A. He was stoned.

"Q. Is sabbath-breaking a great sin in the sight of God?--A. Yes. (Ib. p. 104) He who breaks the sabbath robs God of his own; for the day is the Lord's."

[F] "Were it now revealed to us," says Mr. Jones (ib. p. 180), "that the most extensive system of instruction which we could devise, requiring a vast amount of labor, and protracted through ages, would result in the tender mercy of our God in the salvation of the soul of one poor African, we should feel warranted in cheerfully entering upon our work, with all its costs and sacrifices; for our reward would exceed all our toil and care above the computation of any finite mind." Badly educated, misguided, we believe Mr. Jones to be; but these are the words of honest, sincere conviction.

[G] For a loan of this book we are indebted to our friend Parker Pillsbury.

[H] "A Catechism of Scripture Doctrine and Practice for Families and Sabbath Schools, designed also for the Oral Instruction of Colored Persons, by Charles C. Jones," 6th edit.; Charleston, 1845. In his preface, Mr. Jones says, "The Catechism has been prepared expressly for the religious instruction of the negroes; and it has been extensively tried and approved by those engaged in that good work." It is unquestionably much more used than any other. It has already passed through six editions. It really merits this position.--For a perusal of this book we are indebted to the kindness of our friend Samuel Brooke, of Ohio.

[I] "Let us ever remember the name that Hagar gave to God, 'Thou God seest me,' and act as in his presence. Let us be afraid to steal or lie or curse, or break the Sabbath, or do any wicked thing. God will see and know."--Jones's "Catechism," p. 28.

"Ought not you to try and keep the fear of God always before your eyes? Do not be tempted to say, as too many wicked people do, 'Oh! nobody will know it; nobody will see it.' Remember that God is always looking at you. He sees all that you do: he hears every word that you say: he knows all that you think about: and he can in a moment strike you dead: he is able to destroy both soul and body in hell. Knowing these things, fear him, so as not willingly to offend him."--Rev. Alexander Glennie's Sermons, p. 32. See also to the same point, Bishop Ives's "Catechism," p. 13, 14, 42.

[J] What a beautiful commentary on this teaching is afforded us by Douglass! ("Narrative," p. 47.) Speaking of his grandmother, he says,--"She had served my old master faithfully from youth to old age. She had been the source of all his wealth; she had peopled his plantation with slaves; she had become a great-grandmother in his service. She had rocked him in infancy, attended him in childhood, served him through life, and at his death wiped from his icy brow the cold death-sweat, and closed his eyes for ever. She was, nevertheless, left a slave,--a slave for life,--a slave in the hands of strangers. And in their hands she saw her children, her grandchildren, and her great-grandchildren, divided, like so many sheep, without being gratified with the small privilege of a single word as to their or her own destiny. And, to cap the climax of their base ingratitude and fiendish barbarity, my grandmother, who was now very old, having outlived my old master and all his children, having seen the beginning and end of all of them, and her present owners finding she was of but little value, her frame already racked with the pains of old age, and complete helplessness fast stealing over her once-active limbs, they took her to the woods, built her a little hut, put up a little mud chimney, and then made her welcome to the privilege of supporting herself there in perfect loneliness; thus virtually turning her out to die"! Who that has read Douglass's account of his grandmother, of which this is a small extract, has not been moved both to pity for the slave, and loathing for slavery? Who has not asked with him, "Will not a righteous God visit for these things"?

[K] A slave may die in consequence of "moderate correction," as that term is understood in some of the Slave States.

The Constitution of Georgia, Art. 4, sec. 12, reads thus (Hotchkiss's "Codification," p. 71, 1845):--"Any person who shall maliciously dismember or deprive a slave of life shall suffer such punishment as would be inflicted in case the like offence had been committed on a free white person, and on the like proof, except in case of insurrection of such slave, and unless such death should happen by accident in giving such slave moderate correction."

[L] Our friend Francis Jackson procured us this book.

[M] Mr. Jones thinks ("Rel. Inst." p. 135), that "the crime of infanticide" among the slaves is "restrained in good measure ... by the moral degradation of the people, that takes away the disgrace of bastardy." We remember hearing from Prof. Greenleaf the account of a successful defence, on this ground, of a female slave in this State, who was tried for committing this offence. A female slave, it was argued, could not feel shame at the birth of an illegitimate child, and therefore her affection as a mother would prevent her from committing the crime. But experience has demonstrated, that a slave-mother may be led to take her child's life from very love itself.

[N] "The General Assembly of the Presbyterian Church recently expelled a minister from both the ministry and the church, for marrying a sister of his deceased wife."--The Church as it is, p. 76.

[O] Colored persons are not competent witnesses on the trial of a white man. Any white man, therefore, can, with perfect impunity, commit any excess whatever upon any slaves, so long as they or their companions alone are witnesses. So carefully does the law guard the honor of the female slave!

[P] The original of this advertisement may be seen at the Anti-Slavery office, Boston, 21, Cornhill, pasted on one side of a copy of the newspaper called "Spirit of Liberty"! How appropriate a heading!

[Q] For this and other advertisements from Boston papers, I am indebted to my friend Wendell Phillips.

[R] We cut this advertisement from the "Boston Daily Republican" of Aug. 30, 1849. It previously appeared in the "Providence Journal."

[S] A writer in the "New Orleans Argus," Sept. 1830, in an article on the culture of the sugar-cane, says,--"The loss by death in bringing slaves from a northern climate, which our planters are under the necessity of doing, is not less than twenty-five per cent"! Our tables prove the same thing. Of the 40,000 slaves annually carried south, only 29,101 are found to survive;--a greater sacrifice of life than that caused by the middle passage!

[T] The Act of 1741, of which this law is in part a revision, reads thus, sec. 45: "Which proclamation shall be published on a sabbath-day at the door of every church or chapel, or, for want of such, at the place where divine service shall be performed in the said county, by the parish clerk or reader, immediately after divine service; and, if any slave or slaves, against whom proclamation hath been thus issued, stay out and do not immediately return home, it shall be lawful for any person or persons whatsoever to kill and destroy such slave or slaves by such ways or means as he or she shall think fit, without accusation or impeachment of any crime for the same."--In those happy days, Father Taylor would not have been called on to thank God, that the man who was on the point of strangling his brother according to law was not troubled by any feeling of sentimentalism!

[U] The Rev. Dr. Furman, of North Carolina, another Baptist clergyman, like Dr. Fuller wrote a defence of slavery. After his death, his legal representative advertised for sale at auction his real estate, and "a library of a miscellaneous character, chiefly theological; twenty-seven negroes, some of them very prime," &c. ("The Church as it is," p. 73.)

[V] This point, and the legality of Colonial and State Slavery, are more elaborated in an article called "The Constitutionality of Slavery," printed in the "Massachusetts Quarterly Review;" a purely legal, uninteresting examination, which needs not to be repeated here.

For a more extended proof of the constitutionality of slavery, we refer to Wendell Phillips's very able Review of Lysander Spooner's Essay.

[W] 5 Hen. Stat. 547.

[X] 6 Ibid. 356.

www.ingramcontent.com/pod-product-compliance
Lightning Source LLC
Chambersburg PA
CBHW062008280526
45787CB00005B/2025